W9-AVC-301

CHEF DANIEL BRUCE
Simply New England

Seasonal Recipes That Celebrate Land and Sea

DANIEL BRUCE WITH MAT SCHAFFER

PHOTOGRAPHS BY RON MANVILLE

LYONS PRESS
Guilford, Connecticut
An imprint of Globe Pequot Press

To buy books in quantity for corporate use
or incentives, call **(800) 962-0973**
or e-mail **premiums@GlobePequot.com.**

Text © 2013 Daniel Bruce
Photographs © Ron Manville

ALL RIGHTS RESERVED. No part of this book may be reproduced or transmitted in any form by any means, electronic or mechanical, including photocopying and recording, or by any information storage and retrieval system, except as may be expressly permitted in writing from the publisher. Requests for permission should be addressed to Globe Pequot Press, Attn: Rights and Permissions Department, PO Box 480, Guilford, CT 06437.

Lyons Press is an imprint of Globe Pequot Press.

Project editor: Tracee Williams, Julie Marsh
Text design: Sheryl P. Kober
Layout artist: Melissa Evarts

Library of Congress Cataloging-in-Publication Data

Bruce, Daniel, 1960-
  Chef Daniel Bruce : simply New England : seasonal recipes that celebrate land and sea / Daniel Bruce, Mat Schaffer ; photographs by Ron Manville.
     pages cm
  Summary: "Top chef Daniel Bruce presents delicious, fresh, contemporary New England cuisine through 125 delectable go-to recipes for the home cook"— Provided by publisher.
  ISBN 978-0-7627-8668-8 (hardback)
  1. Cooking, American—New England style. I. Schaffer, Mat. II. Title. III. Title: Chef Daniel Bruce, simply New England. IV. Title: Simply New England.
  TX715.2.N48B767 2013
  641.5974—dc23
                                                        2013019773

Printed in the United States of America

10 9 8 7 6 5 4 3 2 1

CHEF DANIEL BRUCE
Simply NEW ENGLAND

To the women in my life, who fostered my passion for cooking.
To Nana, who demonstrated her love for the family through her countless creations.
To Mom, whose resourcefulness and ingenuity sustained the family.
To Florence for setting me on the path.
And especially to Julianna, my partner and best friend for more than twenty-five years,
without whom this book would never have come into being.

CONTENTS

AUTHENTICALLY DANIEL BRUCE

As a man who has spent his entire career building hotel companies, I understand that there are some basic principles in hospitality that drive the business and give it meaning. The best hotels feel like family. Guests return with the sense that the hotel is a home away from home. Another simple truth: Good food marks occasions and makes memories. When I think back on my own family's celebrations over the years, my memories include meals shared with loved ones. And I'm fortunate because, for many of my family's special occasions, Daniel Bruce has been in the kitchen. Chef Daniel Bruce is an exceptional talent. He came to serve as executive chef at the Boston Harbor Hotel shortly after the hotel first opened its doors a quarter century ago. Daniel has been a visionary leader there. He has been a key player in maintaining the luxury standards that define the Boston Harbor Hotel and ensure that there is no place like it anywhere on earth.

I remember when we recruited Daniel to come work at the hotel. We conducted a nationwide search because we knew we had to find the right person for the job. We wanted a chef who had trained with the best, both here and abroad. We knew the ideal candidate would be both creative and disciplined in technique. We needed someone who had

strong leadership skills but could be a team player. We needed someone with a tireless work ethic. We found Daniel Bruce. How fortunate we were that this young talent taking New York City by storm had decided to come back home. His roots were in New England, and that was where Daniel and his wife, Julianna, had decided they would raise their family.

It is a challenging job to lead as executive chef at a luxury hotel, but Daniel has always loved a challenge and that's probably why he stays. His job is one that never becomes routine. Daniel runs three restaurants, three bars, and in-room dining services. He creates all of the wonderful menus, and oversees catering for all events hosted at the hotel. I recall a wonderful family of Indian heritage whom Daniel worked with on planning their daughter's wedding. The food was the most important element in their celebration. Daniel created a customized menu of authentic Indian cuisine—they said afterward that it was the best Indian food they had ever experienced.

The Boston Harbor Hotel is proud to employ a diverse, multicultural staff. Walking down the line in Daniel's kitchen, you can hear as many as seven different languages. Unwilling to be impeded by language barriers, Daniel has learned all of the languages spoken by his staff. Adding to the Italian and French he learned while training in

Europe, he has picked up Spanish as well as a few basic words in Arabic. His desire to respectfully communicate, connect with, and teach his associates on a daily basis substantiates his leadership abilities as well as his model for excellence.

Daniel makes the Boston Harbor Hotel stand apart, and there is no better example of this than what he has accomplished with the Boston Wine Festival. In 1990, Chef Bruce's desire to showcase his passion for pairing food with wine was the inspiration for creating the Boston Wine Festival at the Boston Harbor Hotel. Of course in typical Daniel style, this signature Boston event is no simple weekend affair. The Boston Wine Festival stretches on for three months every winter. There are numerous evening receptions, brunches, and even a dinner dance. Every week Daniel hosts multicourse, elegant dinners with some of the world's most illustrious winemakers and vineyard owners. In preparation for each dinner, Daniel sits down with the featured wines and tastes them all. With the artistic palette that he is so well known for, he then creates an original menu in perfect harmony with the wine. In twenty-four years, he has never repeated a dish, other than when he celebrated the Festival's twentieth anniversary by bringing back some of his favorite recipes of all time. Quite incredible!

The Boston Wine Festival has become a signature series that defines the hotel in so many ways. It defines luxury and certainly helped the

hotel achieve and retain the prestigious Forbes Five Star award. The cuisine and wine are simply the best, and the service looks extravagant, yet feels thoughtful and gracious. The Festival also defines the hotel in that its attendees become regulars. Like other guests who have discovered our hotel, they have a tendency to return, and when they do, they find that the staff remember them.

As our hotel company grew and we acquired more hotels around the country, I found myself turning to Daniel again and again for his help and guidance. He became a culinary consultant, traveling to hotels, training the chefs, and designing the menus. We identified a few special properties that were appropriate locales to expand his Festival. Daniel has overseen the growth of his Festival in New Orleans, Washington, DC, and Berkeley, California. Like I said, he's tireless.

Daniel has become a friend who is like family. When I can pull him out of the kitchen, we head to the golf course. I like to tell him that he needs to work on his game, but in reality, he's ahead in our ongoing wagers. My wife and I have enjoyed evenings in Daniel and Julianna's one-of-a-kind antique home sharing meals. He even let me cook for him once. All I will say about that humbling occasion is that Daniel was kind with his praise. For Daniel, food is not just food. Food is his life. It's his art, his skill, his tutelage. Above all else, food is how Daniel connects with family and friends. And it is for this reason that I'm excited Daniel has written this cookbook. This cookbook is authentically Daniel Bruce. I can read the energy and enthusiasm in these pages. I can imagine the care with which he created these recipes. Daniel's family already extends beyond his wife and two children. Daniel has made the Boston Harbor Hotel his family, and he has made his network of Wine Festivals his family. Under Chef Bruce's guidance, there is a new generation of chefs emerging—all blazing their own culinary trails, confident that they have learned their trade from one of the best. Now, with the publishing of this book, we can all bring his genius into our home kitchens. Thank you, Daniel, for sharing your passion with us, and thank you for your friendship.

—Rick Kelleher

RESPECTFUL OF MY INGREDIENTS

For as long as I can remember, the forests and lakes of New England have been a source of food for my family and an inspiration for me in the kitchen. I learned early on that, when you live off the land, the seasons govern what's in your refrigerator and freshness isn't an option, it's a necessity. When you depend on Mother Nature, you don't camouflage ingredients with unnecessary extras; you enjoy them for what they are.

When I was growing up, we didn't have a lot, but we never went hungry. I was born in 1960 in Cornish, New Hampshire, a small town on the Connecticut River, with just over a thousand residents and three covered bridges. My parents were kids themselves when they had me: My mom was sixteen and my dad only a year older. Neither ever finished high school. They had three children—me, my sister Debbie, and

my brother Randy—in the space of three and a half years before my mother turned twenty. And another, my brother Deric, fourteen years later. And two more (my half brothers Sean and Charlie), separately, after they divorced.

My dad played in a rock 'n' roll band called the Dead Beats; they drove to gigs in a hearse. For his day job, he worked at a tire company. He loved to hunt and fish and, when I was little, I'd tag along when he went rabbit hunting or partridge hunting or fishing for smelts or brook trout. When I was twelve, we moved to Eustis, Maine, about a thirty-five-minute drive from the Canadian border, in the middle of nowhere. Our new home was a three-room "camp," half a mile from a lake. We had electricity but no plumbing. There was no television, nothing—just a radio that got one station. There was no running water. We used an outhouse.

Randy and I had the task of lugging an old five-gallon, metal milk jug to a spring a mile and a half away, where we'd fill it up with drinking water. We used to put it on a sled—an orange Flexible Flyer—that we'd drag down the dirt road and then out on the paved main road and then onto another dirt road to get to the spring. Once it was full, we'd have to haul it all the way back. It was heavy. We used to try to take shortcuts through the woods but, inevitably, the sled wouldn't make it through all those trees.

That summer, my dad became a registered Maine hunting guide. Whatever he'd kill or catch, we'd eat: perch, pike, salmon, deer, bear, moose, hare, grouse, and woodcock. We also had a little garden out back with a too-short growing season.

My dad made no money. We were a family of four at that time and, if I remember correctly, he brought home five thousand dollars a year or something like that. We couldn't afford to buy a can of tuna, but we could always dig some worms and go down to the lake and fish for pickerel. My mom used to make PLTs—pickerel, lettuce, and tomato sandwiches—for my lunch box. Pickerel are very bony, so my mom used to poach them and chop them up until the bones were so small you could eat them. You know how kids like to trade lunches at school? Well, they never wanted to trade with me once they found out my lunch box was filled with mayonnaise sandwiches and baked bean sandwiches and PLTs.

I can't remember a time that I didn't want to cook. My mom tells me that when I was three years old she saw me drag a chair across the kitchen floor to climb up on a counter to get to a cupboard I couldn't reach, to pull down the ingredients for some no-bake cookies she used to make.

My mother's mother, my Nana S (for Surrell), is a great cook. My mother's parents were more like my parents—she was only thirty-eight and Gramps forty-one when I was born. We spent a lot of time at their house—it was a mobile home, which was a really big thing back then. There was a magical feel in the kitchen. There was always a chicken in the crockpot or a pot of baked beans in the oven—the beans, made with salt pork and onions, smelled so good. And shelves and shelves of canned everything—elderberry jam, piccalilli, sweet slab pickles—that my grandmother put up herself. My Gramps was a guy who could make anything out of anything. We used to tap maple trees with our own wooden spouts that he'd carved himself. We'd collect the sap in old coffee cans and boil it down on a woodstove. The maple syrup had a wonderful, smoky edge.

When I was sixteen, my mom and my dad separated and my sister, my brothers, and I moved with my mom to Skowhegan. It's a town on the Kennebec River that's most famous as the home of Margaret Chase Smith, the first woman to be elected to both the US House and Senate. My mom got a job waitressing at Whittemore's Restaurant. It was a step up from a diner—a family-owned place that served breakfast, lunch, and dinner. They were looking for a busboy, so I took the job. But I hated the dining room; I found the kitchen much more exciting. I wanted to be a dishwasher.

Two weeks later a pot-washing job opened up at The Candlelight, the only fine-dining restaurant in town. I remember walking into the back entrance and there was a line of pots from the door all the way to the kitchen's pot sink; I never knew a restaurant could have so many pots. And every one was burned. The old pot washer, who'd been promoted to dishwasher, said to me, "Congratulations, I hear you've got the job." And I said, "No, I'm here to interview." And he said, "No, no, you've got the job. You can get started right away so we can see how you do."

Well, I'm telling you I couldn't believe the condition of those pots. It took me two days to clean them all. And I promised myself that if I ever became a cook, I would never burn a pot. And I never have. Just the other day, one of my stewards said to me, "Chef, I love when you cook," and I said, "Why?" And he said, "Because you never burn, you never stick, it's so easy to clean up after you." And I laughed, because it all dates back to my days as a pot washer in Skowhegan.

The owner of The Candlelight, a woman named Florence Blaisdell-Sterns, liked my work ethic; I worked almost as much as she did. In my junior and senior years of high school, I worked there full-time. When the pot-washer-turned-dishwasher left, I took on his job to make the extra money. When things got busy, I wouldn't punch out, I'd just keep working. And then they let me do salad prep—you know, those salads with shaved carrots and onions on top served in wooden bowls with bottled dressings? I loved it. And I wanted to do more.

In my off time I used to go fishing, hunt, and forage for edible wild plants—fiddleheads, wild ramps, elderberries, pussy willow, cattails, highbush cranberries. *Stalking the Wild Asparagus* by Euell Gibbons and Bradford Angier's *Field Guide to Edible Wild Plants* were my bibles. I'd look through those books and I'd realize that I had seen and could locate many of the plants they described. Most of my family

didn't want to eat much of what I brought home. Only my sister (and, by the way, she's still alive) trusted me. But when I'd go foraging for wild alpine strawberries or raspberries and come back and make strawberry short-cake or muffins or pancakes, then they ate.

After I had worked at The Candlelight for a year, Florence asked me if I wanted to move in with her; she knew my mom was struggling. She had three daughters and considered me the son she'd never had. One day she said to me, "You love cooking; you should go to cooking school. I can get you a low-interest loan from the Rotary Club and take you down to Johnson & Wales University in Providence and you can apply." And she did and we did and the next thing I knew, I was at Johnson & Wales.

After cooking school, I entered an apprentice program at a restaurant in Massachusetts where I met a visiting chef from Italy who invited me to work for him in Liguria. I'd never been on a plane—or even seen an airport. After two life-changing years in Europe, I returned to America where, thanks to my Italian mentor, I landed a job at Le Cirque.

At Le Cirque I worked alongside the legendary Alain Sailhac and met my wife, Julianna—but that's another story.

Two years later, when Sailhac left to become executive chef at the 21 Club, I went with him and, a year later, when he left 21, I was named executive chef. I was twenty-seven. There were guys in the kitchen that had been working on the line there longer than I had been alive.

I worked at 21 for a year. Management wanted to keep the menu exactly the same but, since this was my first chef's job, I wanted to be creative and show what I could do. The job was for an older chef at the end of his career, not for a new chef trying to launch his career. I was never going to be "Daniel Bruce, the chef"; I would only be "Daniel Bruce, the chef at 21 Club."

Plus, I missed New England. So when Francois Nivaud, general manager of the new Boston Harbor Hotel, approached me about the executive chef's position, I drove up to Boston. Long story short, I got the job and, almost twenty-five years later, I'm still here.

The hotel is a 24/7 operation with two restaurants—Meritage, our wine-centric fine-dining restaurant, and the more casual Rowes Wharf Sea Grille, which specializes in New England cuisine. There are also three bars, room service, and on- and off-site catering. I do the hiring, staff training, menu concepts, and recipes for them all. Plus, there's the Boston Wine Festival, a three-month-long series of winemaker-hosted dinners, seminars, receptions, and brunches that I founded back in 1990—it's the longest-running event of its kind in the country.

I'm involved much more day-to-day than most chefs who've been working at one place for so long. If you've ever visited the hotel, I may have been the one who made your room service omelets. Or lunchtime tuna niçoise. Or mustard-glazed lamb chop dinner. I get in there and roll my sleeves up and cook alongside the guys on the line. I do almost all the meat cutting. I do a lot of the sauces—because sauces are such a key component of good dishes. I go to all my kitchens and make sure every-

thing is running well and help out when necessary. On a typical day, I might get home at nine or ten at night. During the Wine Festival, it's a lot later, generally one or two in the morning.

When I am home, my wife and I share the cooking on a refurbished, nickel-plated, 1926 Clark Jewel gas stove, once used in an old New York City tene- ment house. It has one large oven, one small oven, a broiler,

a bun warmer, and six starburst-style burners. What's for dinner? When I go to the store, I pick up different ingredients based on what looks freshest, what's reasonably priced, and what strikes my fancy; there's no real forethought about what I might actually make. When it's time to eat, I open the fridge, see what I have, and work from there.

My mother's mother, who is now ninety-three, remains an influ- ence. She's all about seasons and fresh ingredients and making every- thing from scratch. Nana S is a simple cook. She lets her ingredients speak for themselves; she would never consider anything else. I think that's why my food is minimalistic in its approach. I believe lobster should taste like lobster and duck should taste like duck. I have the knowledge and technical expertise to make almost anything taste good, but on a basic level I can't do that—instead I allow the ingredients to dictate the preparation.

It's difficult to describe the special appreciation you feel when you don't have something and then you do. That's why I have such respect for the ingredients that come into my kitchen, many of which I never knew existed when I was growing up. The only cheese I knew about was cheddar. We never heard of curry or cumin. The only tropical fruit I remember was the occasional pineapple. But the ingredients we did have were certainly the freshest that we could find.

That's one reason why the woods remain a big part of my life. I just love going out and taking foods from the source. At least once a week, from April to November, I get up in the early, early morning to forage for wild mushrooms. I've located hundreds of patches across New England within several hours' drive of my house, where I know I can find mushroom varieties like chicken mushrooms, hen-of-the-woods, chanterelles, morels, and black trumpets. Bringing back anything less than fifteen pounds is a wasted trip.

Mushrooming is a solo thing. I like to say that a mushroom patch is like a great fishing hole—you show someone that fishing hole and the next time you come back, there's no fish. Because one person tells somebody, and they tell somebody else. But trust me when I say that there's nothing more satisfying than coming home and whipping up a mushroom omelet with mushrooms you just picked yourself. With herbs from your garden or window box and maybe eggs from the local farmers' market.

That's what this book is all about. Dishes that are respectful of their ingredients and simple to prepare. These are the dishes I cook at home, that I share with my family and with my friends. Some recipes date back to my childhood and others are from throughout my career, including my years at the hotel. Some people tell their stories through photographs and videos; I tell mine through recipes. From the tapioca pudding I perfected as an eleven-year-old to the pasta primavera I used to court my wife to the mushroom soup inspired by my foraging.

There are no lengthy preparations and nothing to stress you out. Great food doesn't have to be complicated. These are dishes I make over and over again because they taste good and they work. I hope they will become part of your personal culinary history as well.

Daniel Bruce

—Daniel Bruce

MY KITCHEN ESSENTIALS

My home kitchen is probably stocked very much like your home kitchen. The only difference may be a few ingredients that I consider essential. They make a world of difference in preparing these recipes as well as many others.

STOCKS

I always have stocks in the freezer. They are not difficult to prepare. Make sure you use cold water and reduce the heat as soon as the stock comes to a boil. That will ensure a clear stock.

Chicken Stock

4 pounds chicken bones (ask your butcher) or chicken wings
12 cups cold water
1 onion, peeled and chopped
1 carrot, peeled and chopped
2 celery stalks, peeled and chopped
4 bay leaves
3 sprigs fresh thyme
12 white peppercorns

Rinse the bones or wings in cold water, then place them in a pot with the water, onion, carrot, celery, bay leaves, thyme, and peppercorns. Bring to a boil, then reduce the heat and simmer, skimming as necessary, for 60 minutes. Strain and discard the solids. Cool completely, then refrigerate the stock (if you're going to use it within 3 days) or freeze it in covered containers. Make sure to leave enough room in the freezer containers to allow the stock to expand.

Makes 2¼ quarts

Vegetable or Fish Stock

1 leek, stem removed, split in half lengthwise, thinly sliced and washed
    thoroughly
2 carrots, peeled and thinly sliced
2 celery stalks, thinly sliced
1 onion, peeled and thinly sliced
2 bay leaves
4 sprigs fresh tarragon
½ pound button (or shiitake) mushrooms, thinly sliced
12 white peppercorns
12 cups cold water

Place the leek, carrots, celery, onion, bay leaves, tarragon, mushrooms, and
peppercorns in a large pot with the water. Bring to a boil, then reduce the
heat and simmer, skimming as necessary, for 35 minutes. Strain and discard
the solids. Cool the stock completely, then refrigerate it (if you're going to use
it within 5 days) or freeze it in covered containers. Make sure to leave enough
room in the freezer containers to allow the stock to expand. (If you want to
make fish stock, add a pound of fish bones to these ingredients.)

Makes 2¼ quarts

SALT AND PEPPER

At home I use coarse salt, sea salt, and regular table salt, depending on
the dish. I like to use coarse salt (usually kosher) for salads, meats, and
curing—situations where I want the salt to penetrate slowly. I use sea
salt for almost all my seafood and fish dishes. And I use iodized table
salt for seasoning at the table and salting cooking water. Of course, in a
pinch they can be interchangeable.

I'm a big fan of white pepper because it's more subtle and doesn't
change the color of the foods I'm cooking. But I also use cracked black
pepper over salads, red meat, and darker-colored dishes. Whether you're
using white or black pepper, whenever possible grind it yourself. Previ-
ously ground peppers lose their flavor quickly.

Season to your palate. When it comes to salt and pepper, everyone
has his or her personal taste and tolerance. Season judiciously. You can
always add more salt and pepper to a dish, but you can't take them out
once they're in.

HERBS

It's always best to use fresh herbs—their flavors, colors, and aromas all contribute to the finished dish. These days fresh herbs are available in every supermarket, and even during a New England winter, you can grow herbs in a kitchen window. You know yourself that dry herbs have a different flavor than fresh. But if you must use dried herbs, make sure they've been purchased as recently as possible. When's the last time you cleaned out your spice rack?

OILS

I use olive oils almost exclusively in my cooking, including some of my desserts. Save your fragrant (and pricy) extra-virgin for salad dressings and as a garnishing drizzle; use your less expensive pressings and blends for the heavy lifting, such as sautéing, searing, and frying.

NUTS

Because all nuts contain oil, they can go bad—or lose their flavor—surprisingly quickly.

To get the most out of nuts, bake them very briefly—8 to 10 minutes on a cookie sheet in a 300°F oven—before you use them in a recipe. Or toast them quickly in a dry sauté pan over medium heat, just until they begin to release their aromas.

COOLING

As you will see in this book, I use ice baths frequently to stop the cooking process of many vegetables and maintain their vibrant colors. But I also cool other ingredients—such as potatoes, mushrooms, and fruits—without water, because they're porous and water will change their texture. If you do use an ice bath, make sure you dry the ingredients before proceeding with the recipe.

HEATING

You'd be surprised how many stoves are out of calibration. Invest in an oven thermometer. They're inexpensive and indispensable for ensuring that all your dishes are baked at the correct temperature.

BREAKFAST

Growing up in New England, breakfast was always a big part of the day. You could smell the bacon frying when we were getting out of bed. My brothers and sister and I would run down the stairs to see what else was cooking. Even as an adult, the anticipation of what's for breakfast can motivate you in the morning.

Granola

I've been making this recipe at the hotel for the last twenty-three years. It's great by itself or with yogurt or fresh berries.

3 cups instant oats
1½ cups wheat germ
1 cup shredded coconut
½ cup walnuts
½ cup pecans
½ cup toasted almonds
1 teaspoon cinnamon
¼ cup safflower or canola oil
½ cup peanut butter
2 tablespoons honey
1½ teaspoons vanilla extract
½ cup raisins

1. Preheat the oven to 300°F.

2. In a large bowl, mix together the instant oats, wheat germ, coconut, walnuts, pecans, almonds, cinnamon, oil, peanut butter, honey, and vanilla.

3. Arrange the mixture in two shallow roasting pans. Bake for 40–45 minutes or until lightly toasted, gently tossing the pans halfway through cooking.

4. Stir in the raisins, cool to room temperature, and serve. (Leftovers will keep for two weeks in a tightly covered container.)

Serves 8

Farmhouse Chive Biscuits

I learned this recipe from an eighty-five-year-old Rhode Island woman named Mrs. Aldrich, who taught me how to play whist—and to make these biscuits—while I was studying at Johnson & Wales. To make these biscuits as flaky as they should be, blend the butter into the flour with your fingers, pressing the butter into almond-like shapes that scatter throughout the flour. The idea is to preserve little bits of butter throughout the flour.

1½ cups all-purpose flour
1 tablespoon baking
   powder
1 teaspoon sugar
½ teaspoon salt
6 tablespoons (¾ stick) cold
   butter
¼ cup chopped chives
⅓ cup milk
1 egg, beaten

1. Preheat the oven to 375ºF.

2. Sift the flour, baking powder, sugar, and salt into a mixing bowl.

3. Cut the butter into thin slices and, using your fingers, blend it into the flour. Do not overmix! When the butter has been thoroughly distributed in the flour, stir in the chives.

4. Make a well in the middle of the flour mixture and pour in the milk and beaten egg. Mix together until a soft dough is formed.

5. On a well-floured work surface, roll out the dough ¾ inch thick. Using a 2-inch round biscuit or cookie cutter, cut the dough into eight circles. (The eighth biscuit you'll make from dough scraps.) Carefully place the biscuits on a nonstick cookie sheet.

6. Bake for approximately 10–12 minutes or until the biscuits are light brown. Serve immediately.

Makes 8 biscuits

Blueberry Mint Scones

Even non-bakers will find this scones recipe simple to prepare. Make them with an electric stand mixer with a paddle attachment or use your hands—you don't have to worry about overworking the dough. The mint gives these scones a refreshing zip that will surprise your family and friends. Change the fruit around according to the season: strawberries in the spring, then raspberries and blueberries. In the winter, use dried fruit.

1. Preheat the oven to 375°F.

2. In a large bowl, combine the flour, sugar, baking powder, and salt. Add the butter.

3. Using your fingers, rub the butter and dry ingredients together so that the butter softens into thin, pea-sized pieces.

4. Add the cream, egg, blueberries, and mint. Using a rubber spatula, fold together into a sticky dough.

5. Form the dough into a ball and, on a floured surface, roll it out into a 1-inch-thick square.

6. Cut the dough into six equal squares. Cut each square in half on the diagonal, forming a dozen triangles.

7. Arrange the scones on a nonstick or lightly greased cookie sheet.

8. Bake for 12–14 minutes or until light brown.

Makes 1 dozen scones

2 cups sifted cake flour
1 tablespoon sugar
2 teaspoons baking powder
¼ teaspoon salt
8 tablespoons (1 stick) unsalted cold butter, sliced
¾ cup light cream
1 egg, beaten
1 cup blueberries
1 tablespoon chopped fresh mint

Chive and Honey White Corn Bread

Use this corn bread for breakfast, to accompany chowder or chili, as a side dish with poultry, meats, or fish, or for a tasty snack. If you can't find white cornmeal, use yellow.

⅓ cup honey

1⅓ cups milk

½ cup light olive oil

2 eggs

1¾ cups white cornmeal

1⅔ cups all-purpose flour

1½ teaspoons baking powder

½ teaspoon salt

1 bunch chives, trimmed and chopped

1. Preheat the oven to 350°F.

2. In a large bowl, thoroughly combine the honey, milk, oil, and eggs.

3. Sift together the cornmeal, flour, baking powder, and salt. Fold into the honey-milk mixture. Add the chives and mix until smooth.

4. Pour into a lightly oiled 9-inch baking dish or pie plate.

5. Bake until golden brown or until a toothpick inserted in the middle comes out clean, approximately 35 minutes.

Serves 8

Brown Sugar and Walnut Coffee Cake

To make this delicious coffee cake, you'll need a 10-inch bundt pan. To mix the batter, use either an electric stand mixer with a paddle attachment, a handheld electric mixer, or a wooden spoon and lots of elbow grease. Whichever mixing method you choose, your guests will thank you.

Topping

½ cup brown sugar
1 teaspoon cinnamon
¾ cup chopped walnuts

Mix the brown sugar, cinnamon, and walnuts together in small bowl. Set aside.

Coffee Cake

12 tablespoons (1½ sticks) butter, divided
1 cup sugar
1 teaspoon vanilla extract
2 eggs
2 cups all-purpose flour
1 teaspoon baking powder
1 teaspoon baking soda
1 cup sour cream
1 tablespoon additional butter, for greasing the pan

1. Preheat the oven to 350°F.

2. Using an electric stand mixer with a paddle attachment, a handheld electric mixer, or a wooden spoon, cream together ½ cup (1 stick) of the butter, sugar, and vanilla in a mixing bowl. Beat in the eggs, one at a time, until thoroughly incorporated.

3. Sift together the flour, baking powder, and baking soda. Slowly mix into the batter—it will be lumpy. Stir in the sour cream.

4. Butter a 10-inch bundt pan. Pour in half the batter. Sprinkle with a quarter of the walnut topping mix.

5. Melt the remaining ¼ cup (½ stick) butter. Sprinkle the remaining walnut topping mix over the surface of the cake. Spoon the melted butter over the topping.

6. Bake for 40 minutes or until a toothpick inserted into the top of the cake comes out clean.

7. Cool before serving.

Serves 8

Crazy Light Waffles

When my children, Elliot and Charlotte, were growing up, these waffles were their Sunday-morning favorites, topped with fresh strawberries and whipped cream. My kids can't wait for them to come hot off the waffle iron.

Meringue

2 egg whites

1 teaspoon sugar

Place the egg whites and sugar in a small bowl. Whisk together briskly until soft peaks form. Set aside.

Waffles

1¾ cups cake flour

3 tablespoons sugar

1½ teaspoons baking powder

1 cup milk

2 egg yolks

2 tablespoons butter, melted

1 teaspoon vanilla extract

1. Sift together the cake flour, sugar, and baking powder in a large bowl.

2. Create a well in the center of the dry ingredients and add the milk, egg yolks, melted butter, and vanilla. With a fork, combine the ingredients until half incorporated.

3. Using a rubber spatula, fold in the meringue until all the ingredients are just combined.

4. Ladle the batter into a preheated waffle iron, lightly coated with nonstick spray.

5. Cook until golden brown. Serve immediately (with fresh strawberries and whipped cream).

Serves 4

Fluffy Buttermilk Pancakes

I started making these pancakes in college, when I worked overnights in a bakery. My roommate, Jim, worked in an overnight diner. I'd bring home the pancake ingredients, he'd bring home the bacon, and we'd cook these up before class almost every morning to save money.

1. Sift the flour, sugar, and baking powder into a large bowl.

2. Create a well in the center of the dry ingredients and add the vanilla, buttermilk, and eggs.

3. Carefully mix together the ingredients until just incorporated and slightly lumpy.

4. With the tablespoon of butter, lightly grease a griddle or skillet and heat over medium-high heat. Scoop or pour the batter onto the griddle, using approximately ¼ cup for each pancake. Brown each pancake on both sides and serve immediately.

Serves 4

1¾ cups all-purpose flour
3 tablespoons sugar
1½ teaspoons baking powder
1½ teaspoons vanilla extract
⅔ cup buttermilk
2 eggs, beaten
1 tablespoon butter

Ricotta and Lemon Pancakes

For a different take on pancakes, pass up buttermilk in favor of ricotta and lemon. They make a moist, lemony pancake. Don't have ricotta? Use the same amount of sour cream or yogurt.

2 cups fresh ricotta
2 eggs
⅓ cup milk
Juice and zest of 1 lemon
½ cup sifted all-purpose
    flour
3 tablespoons sugar
2 teaspoons baking powder
1 tablespoon butter

1. In a large bowl, thoroughly combine the ricotta, eggs, milk, lemon juice, and lemon zest.

2. Sift together the flour, sugar, and baking powder. Fold into the ricotta mixture.

3. Lightly butter a griddle or skillet and heat over medium-high heat. Scoop or pour the batter onto the griddle, using approximately ¼ cup for each pancake. Brown each pancake on both sides until springy to the touch. Serve immediately.

Serves 4

My Stove

My stove probably has more stories than I do. In 1996 we redid the kitchen in our Victorian. We needed a new stove. But because I cook with professional ranges all the time, I didn't want my stove at home to be similar to what I worked on all day long.

I heard about a man named Preston Stanley, a former Maine lumberjack who renovated old stoves in Nashua, New Hampshire. On a snowy February morning, my wife, Julianna, and I drove up there. Stanley and I hit it off right away. He knew where I had grown up, so we sort of connected with the Maine roots. He said, "Why don't you go out back and take a look?"

The back of Stanley Iron Works was like a graveyard for old ovens, from the 1920s, '30s, '40s, and '50s. But as soon as we saw one in particular, we knew it was for us. It was a 1926 Clark Jewel gas stove plated in nickel. According to Stanley, it had belonged to the porter of a tenement house in New York City—because it was on the first floor, it wasn't badly damaged when the building was torn down.

It had six burners, a bun warmer, a broiler, and two ovens, one large and one small. It needed to be re-nickeled, but it was still expensive. When we left we had to write him a check for half the amount—for a snowy, beat-up old stove. But I didn't think twice. I said to Julianna, "He's from Maine; he's got to be honest." And he was.

White Cornmeal Johnnycakes with Poached Green Apples

Johnnycakes date back to the native people who lived in New England long before Europeans stepped foot on American soil. New Englanders always make johnnycakes with white cornmeal, but feel free to substitute yellow.

Poached Green Apples

2 tablespoons butter
2 green apples, peeled, cored, and thinly sliced
1 tablespoon sugar
⅓ cup apple cider or apple juice

1. Melt the butter in a medium-sized saucepan over medium heat.

2. Add the apples, sugar, and cider or juice. Cover and slowly simmer for approximately 20 minutes until the apples are meltingly soft, stirring occasionally. Set aside and cool.

Yield: About ¾ cup poached green apples

Johnnycakes

¾ cup all-purpose flour
¾ cup white cornmeal
3 tablespoons sugar
1½ teaspoons baking powder
½ teaspoon nutmeg
2 eggs
¾ cup whole milk
1 tablespoon butter

1. In a large bowl, sift together the flour, cornmeal, sugar, baking powder, and nutmeg.

2. Create a well in the center of the dry mix and add the eggs and milk. Using a fork, carefully mix together the ingredients until just incorporated and slightly lumpy.

3. With the tablespoon of butter, lightly grease a griddle or skillet and heat over medium-high heat. Scoop or pour the batter onto the griddle, using approximately ¼ cup for each pancake. Brown each pancake on both sides and serve immediately, topped with the poached green apples.

Serves 4

Bartlett Pear and Nutmeg Fritters with Cider Syrup

The first Bartlett pear trees in America arrived in Massachusetts in 1799. Commonly known in England as Williams pears, they were planted on an estate in Boston owned by a man named Brewer. The estate was later purchased by a man named Bartlett.

Cider Syrup

4 cups apple cider, divided
1 teaspoon cornstarch

1. In a small bowl, combine 2 teaspoons of the cider with the cornstarch. Set aside.

2. In a large, stainless-steel saucepan over medium-high heat, reduce the rest of the cider to 1 cup, approximately 45 minutes to an hour.

3. Whisk the cornstarch mixture into the hot cider. Bring the cider back to a boil, reduce the heat, and simmer for 1 minute.

Fritters

1½ cups all-purpose flour
1½ teaspoons baking powder
3 tablespoons sugar
½ teaspoon nutmeg
⅓ cup milk
1 egg, beaten
1 tablespoon butter, melted
2 Bartlett (or your favorite) pears, cored, quartered, and diced
Oil for deep-frying
¼ cup confectioners' sugar mixed with 1 tablespoon nutmeg

1. Sift the flour, baking powder, sugar, and nutmeg into a large bowl.

2. Whisk in the milk, egg, and melted butter; beat until just smooth. Fold in the pears.

3. In a large pot, heat the oil to 350°F.

4. Carefully drop rounded teaspoons of the dough into the hot oil. Fry until medium brown, approximately 3 minutes, flipping them over midway.

5. Drain the fritters on paper towels. Dust with the nutmeg-scented confectioners' sugar and serve with the cider syrup.

Serves 4

DANIEL'S TIP:
When deep-frying, remember to let the oil return to the necessary temperature between batches.

Charlotte's Vegetarian Red Flannel Hash

Traditionally, red flannel hash is a hearty breakfast dish made by New England farmers using the leftovers of a corned beef boiled dinner from the night before. Since my daughter, Charlotte, is a vegetarian, I came up with this meatless version that tastes just as delicious. It's super simple to prepare—especially if you make the hash the night before and fry it up in the morning. Vegans can easily substitute vegan spread for the butter and skip the eggs.

1 medium-sized red beet
1 medium-sized potato, peeled
1 red onion, peeled
1 carrot, peeled
1 cup brussels sprouts
1 teaspoon salt
½ teaspoon ground black pepper
2 tablespoons butter

1. Place the beet in a medium-sized saucepan over medium heat, cover with water, and gently boil for 45 minutes or until a toothpick is easily inserted into the beet. Remove the beet from the pot, place it in a bowl of cold water, and peel. Cut into large chunks and set aside.

2. Fill a large saucepan with water and bring to a boil. Cut the potato, red onion, and carrot into large chunks and add to the pot. Gently boil for 15 minutes.

3. Cut the brussels sprouts in half. Add the brussels sprouts and beets to the cooking vegetables. Gently boil for an additional 10 minutes.

4. Drain the vegetables, place them in a medium-sized bowl, and lightly mash with a potato masher. Season with the salt and pepper. Refrigerate until cold or overnight.

5. Heat a 10-inch nonstick pan over medium heat. Add the butter. When the butter begins to bubble, add the hash, pressing it down with a spatula to form an even layer.

6. Cook for approximately 10 minutes until the hash lightly browns, stirring occasionally. Or carefully flip the hash after about 5 minutes if you prefer your hash brown on both sides.

Serves 4

Scallion, Tomato, and Cream Cheese Eggie

This is one of my son Elliot's favorite dishes. It's still his "go-to" breakfast on busy mornings.

1 tablespoon butter

¼ cup cream cheese

6 extra-large eggs, beaten

1 scallion, washed, stemmed, and chopped

1 vine-ripened tomato, cut into quarters and sliced

¾ teaspoon salt

¼ teaspoon white pepper

1. In a large sauté pan, melt the butter over medium heat.

2. When the butter bubbles, add the cream cheese, beaten eggs, and scallion.

3. Lower the heat and cook, stirring occasionally, until the eggs begin to set, about 2–3 minutes. Add the tomatoes, salt, and pepper and cook for another 4 minutes or until the eggs are soft and fluffy. Serve immediately.

Serves 4

Poached Eggs "Finnan Haddie"

Finnan haddie is a Scottish dish of creamed smoked haddock that made its way to New England, where it was enthusiastically enjoyed a century ago. Today it's next to impossible to find smoked haddock at most fishmongers and supermarkets. Here's my non-smoked version.

1. In a medium-sized bowl, combine the haddock cubes, salt, and white pepper. Refrigerate for at least 4—and up to 24—hours.

2. In a medium-sized saucepan over medium heat, bring 2 quarts of lightly salted water to a gentle boil. Add the pearl onions and simmer for 5 minutes. Add the potatoes and cook for an additional 5 minutes.

3. Meanwhile, in a separate medium-sized saucepan, heat the cream over medium heat. Be careful not to let the cream boil. Using a slotted spoon, remove the potatoes and onions from the water and add them to the cream. Gently cook the potatoes and onions in the cream for 5 minutes. Add the haddock to the cream mixture and simmer for 5 minutes or until the fish is cooked through and the potatoes are tender. Set aside, keeping warm.

4. Bring the salted water used to cook the vegetables to a gentle boil. Lower the heat to a simmer. Add the vinegar. Break an egg into a small dish or ramekin. Stirring clockwise with a spoon to create a circular movement, stir up the simmering water. Slide the egg into the center of the moving water. This creates "comet shaped" eggs. Do the same with the remaining three eggs.

5. Poach the eggs in the simmering water: 5 minutes for a soft yolk; 7 minutes for medium; and 9 minutes for a hard yolk.

6. Divide the cod and cream mixture into four bowls. Top with the poached eggs, garnish with the chopped chives, and serve immediately.

Serves 4

½ pound skinless, boneless haddock or cod fillet, cut into 1-inch cubes
¾ teaspoon salt
½ teaspoon white pepper
8 pearl onions, peeled
1 medium-sized Yukon Gold potato, peeled and diced
1 cup light cream
1 teaspoon white wine vinegar
4 extra-large eggs
1 teaspoon chopped chives, for garnish

48-Hour Fennel-Cured Salmon

Everyone loves smoked salmon. In my opinion, this homemade fennel-cured salmon is an excellent alternative—on a bagel with cream cheese, with scrambled eggs, or all by itself, with maybe some capers and chopped onion on the side. Ask your fishmonger to remove the tiny pin bones that run down the center of the fish, or do it yourself with tweezers. This recipe is easily divided in half.

½ cup coarse salt

¼ cup granulated sugar

¼ cup brown sugar

½ cup coriander seeds, crushed in a mortar and pestle or with the side of a knife

½ cup roughly chopped fennel fronds

2 tablespoons cracked black pepper

1 (2½- to 3-pound) boneless side of Atlantic or Nova Scotia salmon

1. In a small bowl, combine the salt, sugars, crushed coriander seeds, fennel fronds, and black pepper. Mix together.

2. On a counter, lay out a sheet of plastic wrap twice the width and length of the salmon.

3. Arrange half the curing spices in the shape of the salmon down the middle of the plastic wrap in an even layer.

4. Lay the salmon on top of the curing spices. Cover it with the remaining spices as evenly as possible.

5. Wrap the salmon with the plastic wrap, using additional wrap if necessary to assure the fish is tightly sealed.

6. Place the plastic-wrapped fish on a cookie sheet and refrigerate for 24 hours, draining any fluids that may accumulate. Flip the salmon and refrigerate for an additional 24 hours.

7. After 48 hours total, remove the salmon from the wrap and carefully wipe off the curing spices. Slice thin and serve. (Extra salmon will keep for a week, tightly wrapped and refrigerated.)

Serves 8

Fresh Sage, Pork, and Maple Patties

With all due respect to the country's excellent, professional sausage makers: Once you've made your own sausage patties at home, you'll never buy store-bought again.

3 slices white bread, cut into small pieces, crusts discarded
3 tablespoons maple syrup
2 tablespoons milk
1 egg, beaten
1 pound ground pork, 80% lean
1 tablespoon finely chopped fresh sage
2 teaspoons salt
1 teaspoon sweet paprika
1 teaspoon ground black pepper
1½ tablespoons olive oil

1. In a medium-sized bowl, combine the bread, maple syrup, milk, and egg. Allow to rest for 5 minutes until the bread soaks up the liquids. Mix well with a spoon.

2. Add the pork, sage, salt, paprika, and black pepper to the bowl. Gently mix together, being careful not to overwork the meat. Form into eight evenly sized patties.

3. Brush the patties with olive oil and grill over medium-high heat on a well-seasoned skillet or grill, flipping after 2–3 minutes, until pink inside.

Makes 8 patties, serving 4–6

STARTERS

When I got into the cooking business, first courses were first courses and entrees were entrees. Today appetizers and main dishes are all but interchangeable. My restaurant Meritage has a menu made up entirely of small plates that you mix and match. So while the heading of this chapter reads "Starters," use these dishes any way you'd like.

White Bean, Sun-Dried Tomato, and Basil Dip

Try this dip at your next informal get-together or sit-down dinner party. It's excellent with either Champagne or a still white wine. Your houseguests will never imagine that something so delicious is so easy and inexpensive to make.

1 cup dried great northern white beans
2 cloves garlic, peeled and chopped
1 small carrot, peeled and chopped
1 small onion, peeled and chopped
⅓ cup (packed) sun-dried tomatoes, chopped
⅓ cup olive oil
¼ cup (packed) fresh basil, chopped
½ teaspoon ground coriander
¾ teaspoon salt
¼ teaspoon white pepper

1. In a bowl, cover the beans with 2 cups of cold water and soak overnight.

2. Drain the beans, discarding any extra water, and place in a large saucepan with the chopped garlic, carrot, onion, and 2 cups of water. Cover, bring to a boil over medium-high heat, reduce the heat, and slowly simmer until the beans are very tender, about 1 hour, adding additional water if necessary to keep the mixture moist. Add the sun-dried tomatoes to the pot 5 minutes before you think the beans will be done. Remove from the heat.

3. Cool for 5 minutes, then, using the back of a wooden spoon, begin crushing the beans against the side of the pot until they begin to puree. Beat in the olive oil and basil.

4. Stir in the coriander and season with salt and pepper. Serve with toasted pita chips or slices of toasted baguette.

Serves 8

Grilled Eggplant and Roasted Shallot Dip

Based on the idea of baba ghanoush, this simple, smoky eggplant dip goes well with almost any cracker. When buying eggplant, remember that smaller eggplants have fewer seeds and tend to be less bitter.

1. Preheat the oven to 400°F.

2. Slice each eggplant lengthwise in half and score the flesh side with a small knife, cutting through the flesh to (but not through) the skin in a diagonal pattern. Brush the eggplant halves with olive oil, about a tablespoon of oil for each half.

3. Heat a stovetop grill (or a nonstick sauté pan) over medium-high heat. Grill the eggplant halves until both sides are well marked.

4. Place the eggplants flesh-side down on a lightly oiled cookie sheet. Bake for 30 minutes. Remove from the oven and allow to cool.

5. Meanwhile, place the remaining olive oil in a small sauté pan over medium heat. Add the shallots and garlic and sauté until tender, about 8 minutes. Set aside to cool.

6. Scoop the eggplant flesh out of the skins and into a bowl. Add the shallots and garlic along with the oil they were sautéed in, the vinegar, and the yogurt. Stir briskly with a fork to form a chunky dip—or with a whisk if you prefer a smoother consistency. Season with salt and pepper, garnish with the chopped parsley, and serve.

Serves 4

2 medium-sized black eggplants
⅓ cup olive oil
4 shallots, peeled and thinly sliced
2 cloves garlic, peeled and thinly sliced
2 tablespoons red wine vinegar
¼ cup whole-milk yogurt
¾ teaspoon salt
½ teaspoon black pepper
¼ cup chopped fresh parsley, for garnish

Cheese Sauce–Filled Popovers

Popovers are much easier to make than you think. In fact, if you follow my recipe, they're foolproof. Just be sure to bake extra—they disappear quickly.

Cheese Sauce

1 cup heavy cream
1 teaspoon cornstarch
1 tablespoon water
¼ cup grated cheddar
¼ cup grated gouda
¼ teaspoon white pepper

1. In a medium-sized saucepot over medium-high heat, bring the cream to a boil. Lower the heat so the cream simmers slowly.

2. In a small bowl, combine the cornstarch and water. Whisk the cornstarch mixture into the simmering cream. Stir for a minute or so then stir in the cheeses. When the cheeses are melted, season to taste with the white pepper. Cover and set aside, keeping warm.

Popovers

3 eggs
1 cup milk
1 cup all-purpose flour, sifted
¼ teaspoon salt
¼ cup grated parmesan cheese
10 teaspoons butter, melted

1. Preheat the oven to 425°F.

2. In a large bowl, beat together the eggs and milk. Whisk in the flour and salt. Let the mixture rest for 10 minutes, then stir in the grated parmesan.

3. Meanwhile, place a twelve-mold muffin pan into the oven for 10 minutes to warm.

4. Remove the muffin pan from the oven. Place a teaspoon of butter in ten molds, making sure that the butter coats the bottoms and sides of each mold. Fill each buttered mold two-thirds full with batter.

5. Place the pan in the oven and bake until the popovers are fully risen, slightly crisp, and golden brown, 25–30 minutes.

6. Fill the popovers with cheese sauce and serve.

Serves 10

DANIEL'S TIP:
Do your cheese sauces tend to curdle? Use a touch of cornstarch slurry (cornstarch mixed with water) to stabilize the sauce. Figure ½ teaspoon cornstarch mixed with 1½ teaspoons water per cup of sauce. The acidity in cheese can make cream curdle; a cornstarch slurry will ensure that your sauce is velvety smooth.

Parmesan Cheese Gnocchi

People shy away from making gnocchi because they tend to be dense and heavy. This easy-to-make recipe produces the lightest gnocchi you will ever find. Feel free to substitute another grated cheese for the parmesan in the cheese sauce.

Gnocchi

1 cup water
¼ cup (½ stick) butter
1 cup sifted all-purpose flour
4 eggs
½ teaspoon salt
¼ cup grated parmesan

1. In a saucepan over medium-high heat, bring the water and butter to a boil. Whisk in the flour and continue whisking constantly until the mixture pulls away from the sides of the pan, about 5 minutes. Remove from the heat and allow the mixture to come to room temperature. Beat in the eggs, salt, and grated cheese until well incorporated. Set aside.

2. Fill a bowl with ice water and cover a cookie sheet with paper towels. Set aside. Bring a large pot of salted water to a boil, then reduce to a simmer.

3. Transfer the gnocchi mix into a pastry bag, a disposable plastic pastry bag, or even a large plastic zip-top bag. If you're using a pastry bag, use a large straight tip. With a disposable pastry bag, cut a hole the size of the dime in the tip. If you're using a zip-top bag, cut a hole the size of a dime in one corner.

4. Pipe ½-inch-long lengths of the gnocchi mixture into the simmering water—they should float to the top in about 30 seconds. Let the gnocchi simmer for 2 minutes, then transfer with a slotted spoon to the ice bath. When they sink to the bottom of the ice bath, place the cooled gnocchi on the cookie sheet.

Sauce

1 cup heavy cream
2 tablespoons grated parmesan
½ teaspoon salt
¼ teaspoon white pepper

In a saucepan over medium-high heat, bring the cream to a boil. Stir in the cheese and season with salt and pepper. Remove from the heat and keep warm.

Assembling

1. Preheat the oven to 375°F.

2. Lightly butter a small casserole dish or four individual ramekins. Add the gnocchi and cover with the sauce.

3. Bake the gnocchi for 10 minutes or until the sauce is bubbling. Serve immediately.

Serves 4

DANIEL'S TIP:
I use an ice bath a lot in my cooking, which is as simple as filling a bowl with ice water and resting a strainer in the water. Plunging cooked ingredients into ice water stops the cooking process and sets texture and color. Just be sure to dry the ingredients off with a clean towel before you proceed with the recipe.

Red Bliss Potato and Truffle Oil Pizza

This white pizza celebrates potatoes, parmesan cheese, and truffles. The aroma of the truffle oil when it's drizzled onto the hot pie permeates the room.

5 red bliss potatoes, peeled and thinly sliced (about ¾ pound)

1 teaspoon cornstarch

1 tablespoon water

½ cup light cream

¼ cup grated parmesan cheese

1 teaspoon salt

1 pound pizza dough, either store-bought or homemade (see following recipe)

¼ cup semolina or cornmeal

4 teaspoons white truffle oil

1. Preheat the oven to 450°F.

2. Place the potatoes in a saucepan filled with water and bring to a boil over high heat. Remove and drain the potatoes immediately and arrange on a plate to dry.

3. In a small bowl, mix the cornstarch and water.

4. In a second saucepan over medium-high heat, bring the light cream to a boil. Lower the heat to a simmer, whisk in the cornstarch mixture, and cook, whisking constantly, for 1 minute. Remove from the heat, stir in the parmesan cheese, and season with salt.

5. Roll out the dough into two 10-inch crusts.

6. Place the dough on pizza pans or a cookie sheet, dusted with semolina or cornmeal. Spread the parmesan sauce on the dough. Cover with the potatoes.

7. Bake for 14 minutes or until the crust is brown. Drizzle with truffle oil before serving.

Serves 4

1. In a large bowl, combine the flour, salt, and sugar.

2. In a measuring cup or small bowl, stir together the yeast, water, and olive oil.

3. Pour the yeast mixture into the flour and knead together—for 5 minutes if you're using an electric mixer with a dough hook attachment, or for 10 minutes by hand.

4. Cover the bowl with plastic wrap or a damp towel and let it rest at room temperature for 1 hour.

5. On a floured surface, pat the dough down and form it into two equal-sized balls. Sprinkle the tops with flour.

6. Flatten the balls and roll out into two 10-inch circles, about ¼ inch thick.

Makes two 10-inch thin-crust pizzas

Pizza Dough

2½ cups sifted all-purpose flour
¾ teaspoon salt
1 tablespoon sugar
1 package yeast
¾ cup warm water
2 tablespoons olive oil
½ cup sifted flour

DANIEL'S TIP:
If you're using store-bought pizza dough, let it rest at room temperature for 15 minutes before you roll it out.

Ricotta and Parmesan Filled Eggplant Rollatini with Garden Vegetables and Parsley Oil

When I was asked to do a televised cooking segment with *Ciao Italia* host Mary Ann Esposito on PBS, I immediately thought of this dish that I make for my daughter, Charlotte, who became a vegetarian at eight years old. Don't be put off by the many steps. Once you do the prep work, the final dish comes together in minutes.

Parsley Oil

½ bunch Italian parsley
1 cup olive oil
Pinch of salt

1. Fill a large bowl with ice water. Bring a kettle of slightly salted water to a boil. Blanch the parsley in the boiling water then plunge it into the bowl of ice water. When it's cold, dry the parsley with paper towels. Do not discard the kettle of boiling water or the ice water.

2. In a blender, blend the parsley, oil, and pinch of salt. Strain the mixture into a small bowl and set aside.

Rollatini

1 medium-sized, oval-shaped eggplant
1 teaspoon salt
½ teaspoon pepper
¼ cup olive oil
1 cup ricotta cheese
½ cup grated parmesan cheese
1 egg
1 cup chopped fresh spinach

1. Thinly slice the eggplant lengthwise into twelve to sixteen ⅛-inch slices. Sprinkle the slices with salt and pepper and drizzle both sides with olive oil.

2. In a nonstick 10-inch sauté pan over medium heat, in batches, lightly brown the slices, on both sides, adding additional oil if necessary. Set the slices aside on a cookie sheet.

3. In a small bowl, combine the ricotta, parmesan, egg, and spinach. Season with salt and pepper.

4. Place a tablespoon or so of filling at the bottom of each of the eggplant slices. Roll the slices up like a jelly roll and place in the bottom of a lightly oiled casserole dish. Cover with plastic wrap and refrigerate until needed.

Tomato Sauce

4 plum tomatoes, hulled
1 tablespoon olive oil
1 clove garlic, chopped
4 leaves basil, chopped
¼ teaspoon salt
¼ teaspoon black pepper

1. Blanch the tomatoes in the boiling water until their skins begin to shrivel, about a minute or so. Remove them to the ice water to cool. When they're cool, peel the tomatoes, cut in half, squeeze out the seeds (don't worry if there are a few left), and cut each half into quarters.

2. Heat the olive oil in a medium sauté pan over medium heat. Add the garlic and sauté for a minute or two, being careful not to let the garlic color. Add the tomatoes and basil and sauté for another 2 minutes, until the tomatoes start to break down. Season with salt and pepper. Set aside, keeping warm.

Assembly

4 pearl onions
1 teaspoon olive oil
4 baby zucchini or 1 small
  regular zucchini, cut on
  the bias
Corn from 1 ear of fresh corn
1 teaspoon salt

1. Preheat the oven to 350°F.

2. Cook the pearl onions in the boiling water for 6 minutes. Remove the onions from the water and peel. Set aside.

3. Bake the rollatini for 10 minutes.

4. As the rollatini are baking, heat a 10-inch sauté pan with the olive oil over medium heat. Add the pearl onions, zucchini, and corn; cook until the zucchini is al dente, about 3 minutes. Season with the salt.

5. Reheat the tomato sauce and spoon it into the centers of four plates. Top with the sautéed vegetables and the rollatini, and garnish with a drizzle of parsley oil.

Serves 4

New England Artisan Cheese Pie with Cider-Tossed Salad Greens

If you like a stress-free dish, cool this pie overnight in the refrigerator; it can be easily sliced and reheated just before you are ready to serve. Trust me—it's so rich and creamy, it's worth the wait. I always use locally made New England cheese, but you can substitute your own locally made cheeses. Your pie will be almost (just kidding) as good.

1 10-inch pie shell, baked
  (see blueberry pie recipe,
  page 244)
4 ounces gouda
4 ounces cheddar
2 ounces soft goat cheese,
  crumbled
4 ounces brie, crumbled
4 ounces mascarpone
1½ cups heavy cream
3 eggs
¼ teaspoon salt
½ teaspoon white pepper
1 tablespoon chopped
  chives

1. Preheat the oven to 350°F.

2. Grate the gouda and cheddar into the bottom of the prebaked pie shell. Cover with the crumbled goat cheese, brie, and mascarpone.

3. Beat together the cream, eggs, salt, and white pepper; pour over the cheeses. Sprinkle with the chopped chives.

4. Bake the pie for 45–55 minutes or until the surface is golden brown and a knife inserted in the center comes out clean. Check the pie at the 20-minute mark. If the rim of the crust is getting too brown, carefully cover it with aluminum foil.

5. Remove the pie from the oven and let it cool to room temperature, approximately 1 hour. Slice and serve over mixed greens tossed with green apples, walnuts, and cider vinaigrette.

Mixed Greens Tossed with Green Apples, Walnuts, and Apple Cider Vinaigrette

¾ cup olive oil
¼ cup apple cider vinegar
2 teaspoons honey
¼ cup chopped shallots
1 teaspoon salt
½ teaspoon black pepper
11 ounces salad greens
  (locally grown if possible)
2 green apples, cored and
  diced
½ cup toasted walnuts

1. Whisk together the olive oil, cider vinegar, honey, and shallots. Season with the salt and pepper.

2. In a large bowl, combine the salad greens, diced green apples, and walnuts. Toss with the cider vinaigrette.

Serves 10–12 (leftovers are delicious warmed up)

Pasta Primavera

Pasta primavera changed my life. It all involves a woman named Julianna Ferriter, whom I met in the Le Cirque kitchen in late January 1986. She was a friend of one of the prep cooks; they knew each other from art school. Julianna was living in Brooklyn and had been working as a colorist for Marvel Comics, on comic books like *Spider-Man, Red Sonja, Conan the Barbarian,* and *Mighty Avengers.* I liked her.

I courted her for several months but she always had one excuse or another not to go on a date with me. Finally, she agreed to meet for brunch one Sunday morning in the West Village. I figured she thought if it didn't work out, it would be easy to escape. Well, we ended up spending the entire day together and, when it got dark, she said, "You want to get dinner?"

I didn't know what to say. I had ten dollars in my pocket and no credit card. I couldn't afford a restaurant but I had enough money to put food on the table. So I said, "You want to come over to my place and I'll cook?" We stopped at a little Korean market and picked up some vegetables. Then we went back to my apartment, where I made hand rolled pasta and a chocolate soufflé with raspberry sauce. My cooking must have done the trick because six months later we moved in together, and a year after that we got married. Twenty-seven years later we're still together.

Pasta Primavera

This is the first dish I ever made for my wife—we've been happily married for twenty-six years. If you don't have the time to make the pasta yourself, buy it fresh from the refrigerator case in your local market. Dried pasta won't win you any hearts with this recipe.

Pasta

2 eggs
1½ cups semolina, divided
¼ teaspoon salt
1 teaspoon olive oil

1. In a large bowl, combine the eggs, 1 cup of the semolina, the salt, and the oil. Stir together with your hands until the mixture forms a thick dough. Pat the dough into a 3 x 3 x 4-inch square. Wrap the dough in plastic wrap and refrigerate for 15 minutes.

2. Remove the dough from the refrigerator and slice into ¼-inch-thick lengths. Roll out the lengths as thin as possible using a pasta machine or a rolling pin, dusting your work surface with some of the remaining semolina as needed to prevent it from sticking.

3. Cut the rolled-out dough into ¼-inch-wide strips. Set aside on a cookie sheet or hang on a pasta rack.

1. In a medium-sized sauté pan over medium-high heat, bring the cream to a boil. Lower the heat to a simmer.

2. In a small bowl, dissolve the cornstarch in the water. Stir the mixture into the cream and simmer for 1 minute.

3. Stir in the parmesan cheese and salt. Remove from the heat, cover, and set aside in a warm place.

1. Heat a pot of lightly salted water to boiling.

2. In a large heavy-bottomed sauté pan, heat the olive oil over medium-high heat. Add the pearl onions and sauté for 5 minutes, stirring occasionally, until the onions turn light brown.

3. Add the garlic, zucchini, and mushrooms; sauté for another 5 minutes, stirring occasionally. Add the tomatoes, peas, and basil, and cook for an additional 4 minutes. Season the vegetables with the salt and pepper.

4. Cook the pasta in the boiling water for 3 minutes. Drain the pasta and toss with the parmesan sauce. Divide the pasta onto four plates. Top each plate with some of the vegetables.

Serves 4

Sauce

1½ cups light cream
1 teaspoon cornstarch
2 teaspoons water
½ cup grated parmesan cheese
¼ teaspoon salt

Assembly

3 tablespoons olive oil
12 pearl onions, peeled
1 clove garlic, peeled and thinly sliced
1 small zucchini, stemmed, washed, and cubed
1 cup cremini (or other) mushrooms, cleaned and quartered
2 plum tomatoes, cored and chopped
½ cup sweet peas
6 leaves fresh basil, washed and chopped
½ teaspoon salt
½ teaspoon black pepper

Cape Cod Cakes and Tartar Sauce

Almost every fish cake recipe uses bread crumbs in the batter as a stabilizer—which makes a firm cake. Not these. By dusting the cakes with bread crumbs and letting them sit in the fridge for an hour, the crumbs are absorbed into the fish mixture to form a crust. So when you cut into a finished cake, it flakes apart and melts in your mouth.

1 pound skinless, boneless cod fillets

½ cup mayonnaise

1 tablespoon chopped fresh parsley

Zest of 1 lime, chopped finely (or use a microplane or grater)

½ teaspoon salt

¼ teaspoon white pepper

2 cups panko bread crumbs, divided

3 tablespoons butter

1. Steam the cod in the top of a double boiler over boiling water until it's almost cooked and just turning flaky, approximately 6 minutes. Be careful not to overcook; the fish will finish cooking later. Remove the fish to a cookie sheet and thoroughly cool.

2. Place the cooled fish in a mixing bowl with the mayonnaise, parsley, and lime zest. Season with salt and pepper. Fold together with a spatula.

3. Sprinkle half of the crumbs onto a cookie sheet. Using a large spoon, form the fish mixture into eight balls and place on the crumbs. Sprinkle the remaining crumbs over the cod balls. Refrigerate for 1 hour.

4. Remove the cod balls from the refrigerator and gently press them into patties, dusting as necessary with the remaining crumbs on the cookie sheet to evenly coat.

5. Melt the butter in a frying pan over medium-high heat. Be sure not to crowd the pan—the cakes will expand and stick together if placed too closely together. When the butter bubbles, sauté the patties, in batches, until golden brown, approximately 4 minutes per side, adding more butter if necessary. Serve immediately with tartar sauce.

Serves 4

Mix together the mayonnaise, lemon juice, capers, onion, and parsley. Season with salt and pepper.

Makes ¾ cup tartar sauce

DANIEL'S TIP:
When you add diced, uncooked onions into any dish, lightly salt them first and allow them to rest for 15 minutes. Discard any of the liquid they have thrown off, pat them dry with a paper towel, and then add them to the other ingredients. This extra step mellows the onion's pungency without losing any onion flavor. Taste before you serve and adjust any additional salt the recipe calls for accordingly.

Tartar Sauce
½ cup mayonnaise
1 tablespoon fresh lemon juice
2 tablespoons chopped capers
2 tablespoons chopped onion, sprinkled with salt and allowed to rest for 15 minutes (see Daniel's Tip)
1 tablespoon chopped fresh parsley
Salt and black pepper to taste

Rope-Grown Mussels Steamed in Ipswich Ale, Mustard, and Tarragon

We New Englanders love mussels. Rope-grown varieties tend to be less sandy and plumper, as they are actually grown on ropes above the ocean floor. This is a simple recipe that's full of flavor. Serve it with lots of crusty fresh bread for sopping up the broth.

1. Lightly scrub the mussels, removing any beards (the fibrous extension that can protrude from the closed shell). Rinse with cold water.

2. In a saucepan large enough to hold the mussels, over high heat, bring the ale and shallots to a rolling boil. Stir in the tarragon leaves, mustard, salt, and pepper.

3. Add the mussels. Cover immediately and simmer for 5 minutes or until all the mussels open, being careful not to overcook.

4. Divide the mussels and their broth among four deep bowls and serve.

Serves 4

2 pounds rope-grown mussels

2 cups Ipswich ale (or your favorite ale)

4 shallots, peeled and thinly sliced

3 sprigs fresh tarragon, leaves only

3 tablespoons Dijon mustard

¼ teaspoon salt

¼ teaspoon black pepper

Maine Lobster and Sweet Corn Cakes

You'll need to use freshly picked corn for this end-of-summer dish. Frozen or canned corn can't compare to kernels right off the cob.

1 cup sour cream

1 egg, beaten

1 teaspoon baking powder

¼ cup sifted all-purpose flour

1 tablespoon chopped chives

½ teaspoon salt

Kernels cut from 2 ears of fresh corn (see Daniel's Tip)

3 tablespoons butter, divided

¼ pound roughly chopped lobster meat

1. In a bowl, combine the sour cream, beaten egg, baking powder, flour, and chives. Season with salt. Stir in the corn kernels.

2. In a 10-inch nonstick sauté pan over medium-high heat, melt half the butter. In two batches, drop rounded tablespoons of the batter into the butter to form silver-dollar-sized cakes, being careful not to overcrowd the pan (the cakes will expand). Gently brown on both sides, about 3 minutes per side. Add the remaining butter before your second batch.

3. Remove the cooked corn cakes to a warm platter, garnish with the lobster meat, and serve.

Makes about 12 cakes, serving 4

DANIEL'S TIP:
When cutting corn kernels right off the cob, rub the shucked ear of corn with a clean, damp dishtowel to remove any silk. Place the cob flat on a cutting board and slice the kernels from stem to tip, being careful not to cut into the fibrous cob. This will keep the kernels from scattering.

Griddled Cheddar, Scallion, and Maine Shrimp Quesadilla

Everyone likes quesadillas. The filling ingredients are so easily substituted. For example, omitting the shrimp and adding spinach in this recipe makes it a great vegetarian option. Experiment, have fun, and use ingredients you love.

1. In a small saucepan over medium-high heat, melt 1 tablespoon of the butter. When it bubbles, add the shrimp and salt. Cook, stirring occasionally, for 4–5 minutes, until the shrimp is tender. Set aside.

2. Place the tortillas on a clean work surface. Sprinkle an equal amount of cheese on the bottom half of each tortilla, followed by the scallions and shrimp.

3. Gently fold the top halves of the tortillas over the bottom halves to form eight half-moon-shaped quesadillas.

4. Melt the remaining butter. Brush the quesadillas with the melted butter and griddle in a hot skillet or sauté pan over medium-high heat until golden brown, about 3–4 minutes per side. (Conversely, skip the melted butter and bake the quesadillas in a preheated 375°F oven or on top of a preheated grill for a healthier but no less tasty version.)

5. Cut the quesadillas into pie-shaped wedges and serve.

Serves 8

4 tablespoons (½ stick) butter, divided
1 pound peeled, baby Maine shrimp (or other peeled small shrimp)
¼ teaspoon salt
8 (10-inch) soft flour tortillas
2 cups grated Vermont cheddar cheese
2 bunches scallions, stemmed and roughly chopped

DANIEL'S TIP:
If you can find them, freshly caught Maine shrimp are available only in January and February. They're no bigger than your thumbnail but incredibly sweet and delicious.

Lemony Jonah Crab Cakes with Celery Root Mayonnaise

Jonah crab is a species that's caught along the East Coast. It has a subtly sweet, fresh taste that makes it excellent for crab cakes. When you mix the crabmeat together, be gentle—you want to keep the pieces of crabmeat as whole as possible.

Crab Cakes

8 ounces Jonah crabmeat (or any fresh local crabmeat)

½ cup mayonnaise

2 tablespoons finely chopped chives

Zest of 1 lemon, chopped finely, or use a microplane or grater

½ teaspoon salt

Pinch of cayenne pepper

1 cup bread crumbs

4 tablespoons (½ stick) butter

1. Lightly squeeze the crabmeat to remove excess moisture and place it into a bowl with the mayonnaise, chives, and lemon zest. Season with the salt and cayenne pepper. Gently fold the mixture together with a spatula.

2. Place the crumbs on a cookie sheet. Divide the crabmeat mixture into four patties and gently coat the patties with the crumbs. Refrigerate the crumbed patties for an hour.

3. Melt the butter in a nonstick 10-inch sauté pan over medium-high heat. When the butter bubbles, sauté the crab cakes until golden brown on both sides, about 3 minutes per side. Serve immediately with celery root mayonnaise.

Celery Root Mayonnaise

1 small celery root

⅓ cup mayonnaise

½ teaspoon chopped fresh thyme

Salt to taste

1. Peel and cube the celery root. Cook it in boiling water until very tender, about 15 minutes.

2. Remove the celery root from the water and cool for 10 minutes.

3. In a food processor or blender, puree the celery root, mayonnaise, thyme, and salt. Refrigerate until ready to use.

Serves 4

Pan-Seared Diver Scallops and Cider Butter Sauce

Ask your fishmonger for day boat or diver scallops. They contain little or no extra water, which makes them easier to sear. Look for scallops that are translucent, not white. White scallops most likely have been frozen.

1 cup white wine

1 cup apple cider

1 small onion, peeled and diced

4–6 white peppercorns

1 bay leaf

2 sprigs fresh thyme

4 tablespoons (½ stick) butter

¼ teaspoon salt

12 large (10–20 count per pound) sea scallops

Sea salt

White pepper

4 teaspoons olive oil, divided

1. In a saucepot over medium-high heat, bring the white wine, apple cider, diced onion, peppercorns, bay leaf, and thyme sprigs to a boil. Cook until the liquid has been reduced to slightly more than ½ cup.

2. Strain the sauce back into the pot, discarding the solids, and let cool for 5 minutes. When the liquid is lukewarm to the touch, place the pot over low heat and whisk in the butter. When the butter has melted and the sauce has slightly thickened, stir in the salt. Remove the pan from the heat and keep warm.

3. Remove the scallops' abductor muscles—those little tabs on the side—and set aside.

4. Heat a 10-inch nonstick pan smoking-hot on highest heat.

5. Lightly sprinkle the tops and bottoms of each scallop with the sea salt and white pepper.

6. Add half the oil to the pan. When the oil starts to smoke, place half the scallops in the pan. Sear both sides of the scallops golden brown, about 2–3 minutes per side. Remove the scallops from the pan and keep warm. Add the remaining oil to the pan and heat until smoking. Cook the remaining scallops.

7. Divide the scallops among four plates and garnish with a generous drizzle of apple cider butter sauce.

Serves 4

DANIEL'S TIP:

When searing scallops, once you put them in the hot pan, don't move them until you can see the edges turning brown. And don't lower the flame. This will give you scallops with that nice caramelized color—the way you like it.

Cooking in Italy

My approach to Italian cuisine was shaped by Angelo Paracucchi, a chef I met when I was working at my first post-graduation job, at a restaurant called the Castle in Leicester, Massachusetts. It was built like a sixteenth-century castle with turrets and a moat and served a menu of old-fashioned European dishes like lobster thermidor, tournedos Rossini, and steak Diane, punctuated with Albanian dishes that reflected the owners' background. I was the senior apprentice.

The Castle participated in a visiting-chef program, run by Johnson & Wales. In the summer of 1983, they brought in Paracucchi, who, at the time, was one of the most innovative chefs in Italy. He cooked an amazing meal that I remember to this day. The first course was chilled lobster with tomato-orange vinaigrette, which was followed by pheasant consommé with little bowtie pasta made by his wife, Francesca. Then roasted guinea hen with garlic-sautéed rabe, roasted potatoes, and meat jus for the main course. I was just blown away. I couldn't believe this was Italian food.

When Paracucchi went back to Italy, he asked me if I'd like to come work with him at his restaurant in Marinella di Sarzana on the Ligurian coast. Not only had I never been on a plane, I'd never seen an airport. I didn't speak a word of Italian—I honestly thought *ciao* meant "food."

The restaurant was called Locanda dell' Angelo. It was considered one of the best restaurants in Italy, which was saying a lot. Paracucchi insisted on the freshest, most seasonal ingredients: vegetables grown by local farmers, locally harvested white truffles and porcini, pasta made minutes before it was dropped into boiling water. I remember one day when a hunter brought in a freshly killed wild boar, slung over his shoulder, for us to butcher and cook. I realized that Paracucchi was doing what my family did but on a much higher level. Needless to say, you couldn't get me out of the kitchen.

Chilled Lobster Salad with Tomato-Citrus Vinaigrette

Here's a great summer lobster salad that's much lighter than the traditional version found all over New England. The idea for the dressing came from Angelo Paracucchi, a mentor of mine whom I worked with in Liguria, Italy. He created an olive-oil-based sauce with tomatoes and oranges that opened my eyes to the many possibilities of Italian cuisine.

1. Cut each lobster tail into halves lengthwise. Remove any stringy entrails, located toward the top of the tail.

2. Core the tomatoes. Cut each tomato in half.

3. Zest the orange with a microplane or grater. Cut the orange in half and juice, discarding any seeds.

4. In a blender or food processor, combine the tomatoes, orange zest, orange juice, shallots, salt, and pepper. When the mixture is smooth, slowly pour in the olive oil. Pour the tomato-orange vinaigrette through a strainer and set aside.

5. Divide the watercress among four plates. Top each plate with two lobster tails and a ladle of dressing. Sprinkle with chopped chives and serve immediately.

4 fresh Maine lobster tails, cooked and chilled
2 fresh plum tomatoes
1 orange
2 shallots, peeled and cut in half
½ teaspoon salt
¼ teaspoon ground white pepper
¼ cup olive oil
2 bunches watercress, trimmed, washed, and dried
1 small bunch chives, chopped

Serves 4

Patriot Chicken Wings

I made these wings in 2002 on *Live! with Regis & Kelly* in a segment on Super Bowl eating—two days before the New England Patriots appeared in Super Bowl XXXVI. Howie Mandel filled in for Regis Philbin that morning. The Patriots beat St. Louis 20–17.

1. Preheat the oven to 450°F.

2. In a large pot, bring 3 quarts of salted water to a boil. Add the chicken drummettes, and simmer for 10 minutes. Strain and cool.

3. In a large saucepan over medium-high heat, bring the maple syrup, lager, chile paste, malt vinegar, and salt to a slow boil.

4. Dissolve the cornstarch in the water and whisk into the maple syrup mixture. Simmer for 1 minute and remove from the heat.

5. Place the wings in a large bowl and toss with three-quarters of the glaze. Place the wings onto a buttered cookie sheet and bake for 18 minutes, or longer if you prefer crispier wings.

6. Sprinkle the wings with the chopped scallions and serve the remaining sauce for dipping. Stock up on extra napkins.

Serves 4–6

24 chicken drummettes
1 cup maple syrup
½ cup New England lager beer
¼ cup sambal or red chile paste (add more if you like your wings spicier)
3 tablespoons malt vinegar
1½ teaspoons salt
3 tablespoons cornstarch
3 tablespoons water
1 bunch scallions, ends removed and chopped, for garnish

SOUPS

I probably get more compliments on my soups than anything else I make—either in the hotel restaurants or at home. It amazes me that more people don't try to make their own soups, because—if you follow a few simple rules—they couldn't be easier to prepare. When you smell a pot of soup simmering on the kitchen stove, you know you're in for a delicious treat.

Easiest Wild Mushroom Broth

If you can boil water, you can make this soup.

1½ pounds assorted
   wild mushrooms (such
   as oysters, shiitakes,
   portobellos, chanterelles)
1 leek
2 bay leaves
3 thyme sprigs
1 small onion, peeled and
   chopped
2 small celery stalks,
   trimmed and chopped
16 cups water (1 gallon)
1½ teaspoons salt
½ teaspoon white pepper
1 tablespoon truffle oil, for
   serving

1. Clean the mushrooms (see Daniel's Tip) and cut them into quarters.

2. Remove the roots from the leek, then split it lengthwise and thinly slice into half-moons. Drop the slices into a bowl of water to dislodge any sand, then remove and pat dry with paper towels.

3. Place the mushrooms, leek, bay leaves, thyme sprigs, chopped onion, celery, and water into a large kettle. Bring to a boil, lower the heat, and simmer for approximately 3 hours or until the liquid has been reduced by two-thirds.

4. Season with salt and pepper. Serve with a drizzle of truffle oil.

Serves 6

DANIEL'S TIP:
Never use water to clean mushrooms. Use a mushroom brush or a damp paper towel to lightly rub off any excess debris. Mushrooms are like sponges and will absorb water, which makes them hard to sauté.

White Cauliflower Soup

For this soup, the onions are cooked very slowly, which allows the soup's color to remain white, showcasing the cauliflower.

1. In a large pot over medium heat, melt the butter. Add the onion and cook slowly until very tender, about 10–12 minutes, being careful not to let the onion brown at all.

2. Add the cauliflower. Season with salt and pepper. Cover the pot and cook for 5 minutes, stirring occasionally.

3. Uncover the pot and add the chicken stock. Increase the heat, bring to a boil, lower the heat, and simmer, partially covered, for 20 minutes or until the cauliflower is fork-tender.

4. Puree the soup in a blender in batches, or use an immersion blender. Stir in the cream and simmer for an additional 3 minutes. Taste for salt and pepper and serve, garnished with tarragon sprigs and chives or a drizzle of pumpkin oil or aged balsamic vinegar.

Serves 4–6

2 tablespoons butter
1 medium-sized white onion, peeled and sliced
1 head cauliflower, stem and leaves removed, cut into florets
1½ teaspoons salt
½ teaspoon white pepper
3 cups chicken or vegetable stock
1 cup heavy cream
Tarragon sprigs and chopped chives, for garnish
Pumpkin oil or aged balsamic vinegar (optional)

Golden Potato and Leek Soup

I like this dish in early autumn when the potatoes are being harvested. But because it can be served chilled or hot, it's a great soup any time of the year.

4 tablespoons (½ stick) butter

1 white onion, peeled and thinly sliced

2 leeks, white parts and green stems cut into rings and well washed, roots discarded

4 medium-sized Yukon Gold potatoes, peeled and chopped

½ teaspoon ground white pepper

6 cups chicken or vegetable stock

1½ cups light cream

2 teaspoons salt

Chopped chives or caviar (optional)

1. Melt the butter in a large pot over low heat.

2. Add the onion and leeks and cook for 5 minutes, stirring occasionally, being sure that the onions don't color.

3. Add the potatoes, white pepper, and chicken stock.

4. Bring the mixture to a simmer. Cover the pot, leaving the lid slightly ajar, and cook until the potatoes are tender, about 30 minutes.

5. Puree the soup in a blender in batches, or use an immersion blender.

6. Whisk the light cream into the soup and simmer for an extra 3 minutes.

7. Season with salt and serve immediately or let the soup cool, refrigerate, and serve cold, garnished with optional chopped chives or a dollop of caviar.

Serves 8

Parsnip Cider Soup

Parsnips and apple cider are two quintessentially New England ingredients. Years ago many New Englanders would leave their parsnips in the ground through the winter and dig them up with a pitchfork after spring thaw. I'm lucky enough to have a farmer who still does this for me for my restaurants, because spring-dug parsnips are very sweet. But since all parsnips—regardless of when they're harvested—are good, don't worry!

1 large or 2 small leeks
  (about ¾ pound)
2 tablespoons butter
1 small white onion, peeled
  and sliced
2 cups peeled and sliced
  parsnips
¾ teaspoon salt
½ teaspoon white pepper
2 cups chicken or vegetable
  stock
1 cup apple cider
½ cup light cream
2 tablespoons chopped
  parsley, for garnish

1. Remove the stems and green tops of the leeks. Slice the white portions into thin rounds; wash them well to remove any sand, then pat dry with a paper towel.

2. In a large pot over medium heat, melt the butter. Add the leeks and onion and slowly sauté for 5 minutes, stirring occasionally, making sure not to let the onion brown. Add the parsnips and season with the salt and pepper. Add the chicken stock and cider and bring to a simmer. Cook until the vegetables are tender, about 30 minutes.

3. Puree the soup, in batches, in a blender, or use an immersion blender. Return to the pot and stir in the cream.

4. Serve hot or cold, garnished with the chopped parsley.

Serves 4

DANIEL'S TIP:
By starting a soup with onions and butter and then either gently cooking (sweating) or caramelizing the onions over higher heat, you not only determine the final color of the soup, but also bring wonderful depth of flavor to the final product.

DANIEL'S TIP:
For an extra special finishing touch, use a potato peeler to create shavings from a parsnip to the core, heat ½ cup oil to 225ºF, and fry the peelings for about 30 seconds. Place onto a paper towel and season.

Native Fiddlehead and Green Onion Soup

Fiddlehead ferns are a rite of springtime for many New Englanders and appear in local grocery stores from the end of April to the beginning of June. Every spring, growing up, I used to go down to the floodplains of the Connecticut River with my grandparents and pick hundreds of pounds of fiddleheads to sell to local restaurants. This was my grandfather's favorite soup that I made for him. If you don't have access to fiddleheads, you can substitute asparagus. And you can switch out the butter for smoky bacon—which is how my grandfather liked it.

1. Place the fiddleheads in a bowl of water and stir briskly to remove any brown skin that may be clinging to them.

2. In a large saucepot over medium-high heat, melt the butter or, if you're using bacon, render the bacon of its fat.

3. Add the green onions and cook until tender, about 3–4 minutes.

4. Pour in the stock, raise the heat, bring to a boil, and add the fiddleheads and chopped potato.

5. Lower the heat and simmer for 15 minutes or until the vegetables are tender. Season with salt and pepper. Puree the soup in batches in a blender, or use an immersion blender. You can also serve the soup just as it is—which is how my grandfather preferred it.

Serves 8

3 cups fresh fiddlehead ferns

3 tablespoons butter or
  3 slices smoky bacon,
  chopped

1 cup green onions (or
  scallions), trimmed
  of roots and coarsely
  chopped

6 cups chicken or vegetable
  stock

1 medium-sized potato,
  peeled and chopped

2 teaspoons salt

¾ teaspoon black pepper

Creamy Sweet Onion Soup

I like using Vidalia onions because of their sweetness, but for this soup any white onion will do. It's a great way to use up onions that have been sitting around your kitchen too long.

2 tablespoons butter

3 medium-sized Vidalia onions, peeled, cut in halves, and thinly sliced

½ teaspoon chopped garlic

¼ cup white wine

1 medium-sized Yukon Gold or white potato, peeled and diced

2½ cups chicken or vegetable stock

1 thyme sprig

1 bay leaf

1 cup light cream

¾ teaspoon salt

¼ teaspoon white pepper

1. Heat the butter over medium-high heat in a large saucepot.

2. Sauté the onions and garlic until the onions turn a light, golden brown, about 10 minutes, stirring frequently. Lower the heat if the onions begin to darken too much.

3. Add the wine, increase the heat, and reduce the wine by half.

4. Add the potatoes, chicken stock, thyme, and bay leaf. Simmer for 20 minutes, reducing by half.

5. Remove the thyme sprig and bay leaf then puree the soup in batches in a blender, or use an immersion blender.

6. Whisk in the cream and simmer for 3 minutes. Season with salt and pepper and serve.

Serves 8

DANIEL'S TIP:
Never store onions in a plastic bag. Onions like it cool, dry, and dark—use a brown paper bag or mesh cloth bag.

Fresh Corn Chowder

This vegetarian chowder is especially good in summer when the corn is at its peak freshness with a sweet edge. I grew up in the Upper Connecticut River Valley, where there were always miles and miles of corn on both sides of the river. This soup reminds me of those days.

1. Shuck the corn. Rub the shucked ears with a clean, damp dishtowel to remove any silk. Cut the corn kernels off the cobs (see page 58) and set aside.

2. Place the cobs in a large pot with the water. Bring to a boil, lower the heat, and simmer for 30 minutes. Strain and reserve the liquid; remove and discard the cobs.

3. In a second large pot, melt the butter over medium-low heat. Add the onion and gently cook until it turns translucent, about 5 minutes, being careful not to let the onion color.

4. Add the reserved corn stock and potatoes, raise the heat, and bring the mixture to a boil. Lower the heat and simmer for 10 minutes.

5. Add the corn kernels and cream and gently simmer until the potatoes are tender, about 5 minutes.

6. Season with salt and pepper and serve, garnished with the chives.

Serves 6

4 ears sweet corn

5 cups water

2 tablespoons butter

1 large onion, peeled and diced

4 medium-sized Yukon Gold potatoes, peeled and cut into ½-inch cubes

2 cups light cream

1 teaspoon salt

½ teaspoon white pepper

2 tablespoons chopped fresh chives, for garnish

Harvest Vegetable Soup

This soup is wonderful on a crisp fall day. Feel free to substitute your favorite root vegetables for my selections. If you reserve one or two slices of rutabaga and butternut squash, dice them and boil them up separately—they make a great garnish.

1 medium-sized onion

1 medium-sized carrot

1 medium-sized rutabaga

1 small butternut squash, approximately 1 pound

3 tablespoons butter

5 cups chicken or vegetable stock

4 sprigs fresh thyme

1½ teaspoons salt

¾ teaspoon white pepper

1 cup grated cheddar cheese, for garnish

1 cup toasted walnuts, for garnish

Boiled, diced rutabaga and butternut squash, for garnish—see headnote (optional)

1. Peel the onion, carrot, and rutabaga, and cut them into ¼-inch slices. Peel the squash, cut it in half, and discard the seeds. Cut the squash halves into ¼-inch slices.

2. Melt the butter over medium-low heat in a large saucepot. Add the onion and slowly cook until tender, about 5–6 minutes, making sure the onion doesn't color.

3. Add the carrot, rutabaga, and squash slices (reserving 1 or 2 slices of rutabaga and squash should you wish to use them as a garnish—see the headnote). Slowly cook for about 5 minutes, stirring occasionally.

4. Add the chicken stock and thyme sprigs, raise the heat, bring to a gentle boil, then lower the heat and simmer until all the vegetables are soft, about 40 minutes.

5. Remove and discard the thyme. Puree the soup in batches in a blender, or use an immersion blender.

6. Season with the salt and pepper.

7. Serve, garnished with the grated cheddar, toasted walnuts, and optional boiled, diced rutabaga and butternut squash.

Serves 8

Cream of Wild Mushroom Soup

Being a longtime forager, of course I would have to have a wild mushroom soup in this book. Using as many different types of mushrooms as possible adds layers and layers of flavor.

1 pound assorted wild mushrooms (such as oysters, shiitakes, portobellos, chanterelles)
3 tablespoons butter
2 onions, peeled and thinly sliced
1 cup Madeira or Marsala
3 cups chicken or vegetable stock
1 cup light cream
1 teaspoon salt
½ teaspoon black pepper

1. Clean the mushrooms and cut them into quarters.

2. Melt the butter over medium-heat in a large saucepot. Add the onions and sauté until they turn light brown, about 7–8 minutes.

3. Turn the heat to high and add the mushrooms. Cook until the mushrooms release their liquid, about 3–4 minutes, stirring occasionally.

4. Add the Madeira or Marsala and continue cooking over high heat until the liquid is reduced by half, about 5 minutes.

5. Add the chicken stock and bring to a boil. Reduce the heat to medium and simmer for 10 minutes.

6. Whisk in the light cream and simmer for an additional 5 minutes. Remove from the heat and carefully puree the soup in small batches in a blender, or use an immersion blender.

7. Season with salt and pepper and serve. (For a smoother soup, strain the soup through a strainer before serving).

Serves 6

DANIEL'S TIP:
The most flavorful mushrooms available in the supermarket are dried porcini. Rehydrate them in warm water for 15 minutes and use the liquid in place of some of the chicken stock—use 1 ounce of dried porcini per 1 cup of water.

New England Clam Chowder

I've been making this chowder at the Boston Harbor Hotel since the first day I arrived. I wanted an authentic New England chowder that had a refreshing, light texture, without the usual floury consistency. It has never left the menu.

1. Chop the celery and onion into small pieces.

2. Peel and dice the potatoes into ½-inch cubes.

3. In a large saucepot over medium-low heat, melt the butter. Slowly sauté the celery and onion until they soften, about 8 minutes, being careful not to let the onion color.

4. Add the wine, raise the heat, and simmer for 5 minutes.

5. Add the clam juice, bring to a boil, cover the pan, then lower the heat to a simmer. Add the potatoes and cream and simmer until the potatoes are tender and the chowder starts to thicken, about 25 minutes.

6. Stir in the clams, season with salt and pepper, and serve garnished with the chives. Pass the crackers.

Serves 8

2 celery stalks, trimmed

1 large yellow onion, peeled

4 medium-sized Yukon Gold potatoes

2 tablespoons butter

½ cup dry white wine

1½ cups clam juice

2 cups heavy cream

2 cups chopped fresh clams

½ teaspoon salt

¼ teaspoon white pepper

¼ cup chopped fresh chives, for garnish

Oyster or common crackers, for serving

Turkey, Barley, and Tomato Soup

This is my wife Julianna's favorite soup to make the day after Thanksgiving with leftover turkey—but it's good enough to eat all year-round. Using uncooked turkey breast adds to the flavor.

6 whole plum tomatoes (or use a 14.5-ounce can of whole tomatoes)

1 cup tomato juice

1 pound pearl barley (approximately 5 cups)

2 onions, peeled and diced

4 medium-sized carrots, peeled and diced

2 tablespoons olive oil

10 cups turkey or chicken stock

2 pounds boneless, skinless turkey breast (uncooked) or about 4 cups cooked turkey

1 teaspoon salt

½ teaspoon black pepper

8 fresh basil leaves, chopped

1. Core the tomatoes, then place them in gently boiling water for 2 minutes or until their peels begin to wrinkle. Cool the tomatoes in an ice bath, then peel them, cut them in half horizontally, and squeeze them slightly to remove the seeds. Cut each half in quarters. Mix the tomato quarters with the tomato juice and set aside. (If you're using canned tomatoes, coarsely chop, reserving the juice.)

2. Rinse the barley in a bowl of cold water and drain.

3. In a large saucepot over low heat, slowly sauté the onions and carrots in the olive oil until the onions become translucent, about 4 minutes.

4. Raise the heat and add the turkey or chicken stock, the barley, and the tomatoes (either fresh with tomato juice or canned). Bring to a boil. Lower the heat, cover the pot, and simmer for 15 minutes.

5. Cut the turkey into ½-inch cubes. Add the turkey to the soup and simmer for an additional 20 minutes. If using cooked turkey after Thanksgiving, just add and bring to a boil to finish. (For a soupier soup, add an extra cup of stock.)

6. Season with salt and pepper, stir in the basil, and serve immediately.

Serves 16

Yellow Split Pea and Smoked Ham Soup

I remember my mom always making this soup and using ham hocks. My brother and I used to fight over who got the hock and, because I was older and bigger, I usually won. This recipe uses smoked ham and a touch of sage, which adds a wonderful herbal essence. If you can't find yellow split peas (a New England staple), green are fine.

1 teaspoon olive oil

1 carrot, peeled and chopped

1 celery stalk, trimmed and chopped

1 onion, peeled and chopped

1 pound yellow split peas

8 cups chicken stock

½ pound smoked ham, diced

2 fresh sage leaves, chopped

½ teaspoon salt

½ teaspoon cracked pepper

1. In a large saucepot over medium-low heat, heat the olive oil. Add the carrot, celery, and onion; gently cook until slightly tender, about 4–5 minutes.

2. Add the split peas and chicken stock. Raise the heat and bring to a boil then lower the heat, place the cover askew on top of the pot so some of the steam escapes, and simmer the soup for 15 minutes. Stir regularly to prevent sticking on the bottom.

3. Add the ham and chopped sage. Continue to simmer the soup, cover askew, for an additional 15 minutes or until the split peas are tender. Season with salt and cracked pepper and serve.

Serves 6

New England Patriots Chili

This is the perfect tailgate chili; it's equally delicious whether you use ground pork, beef, chicken, or turkey, and it tastes even better the next day. The cocoa adds a wonderful depth of flavor. Serve the chili over rice or by itself.

1. Heat the oil in a large saucepan over medium heat. Add the onions, leeks, and garlic; sauté until tender, about 3–4 minutes. Stir in the chile powder, cumin, black pepper, chile paste, and cocoa powder. Continue cooking for another 2 minutes, stirring frequently.

2. Add the ground meat and cook for an additional 5 minutes, stirring frequently.

3. Add the orange juice, crushed tomatoes, tomato juice, tomato puree, and beans. Stir together and simmer for 35 minutes.

4. Season with salt and serve.

Serves 10

2 tablespoons olive oil
2 red onions, peeled and chopped
2 leeks, white parts and green stems cut into rings and well washed, roots discarded
1 tablespoon chopped garlic
2 tablespoons chile powder
2 tablespoons ground cumin
1 teaspoon black pepper
2 tablespoons Chinese chile paste (or more or less depending on your palate)
2 tablespoons cocoa powder
2 pounds ground pork, beef, chicken, or turkey
½ cup orange juice
1 cup crushed tomatoes
2 cups tomato juice
2 cups tomato puree
1 (8-ounce) can kidney beans, drained
1½ teaspoons salt

SALADS

One of the first dishes I created when I started at the Boston Harbor Hotel was a signature salad of crab, tomatoes, and avocado named for our waterfront location on Rowes Wharf. It's still on the menu twenty-five years later. Salads often fly under the radar but, whether they're cutting-edge or traditional, people still love them.

Sautéed Chanterelle, French Green Bean, and Endive Salad

I made this salad on the *Today* show back in 1994, when the show was hosted by Bryant Gumbel and Katie Couric. It was in celebration of Bastille Day and I thought this would be a great salad with its French-inspired ingredients.

Vinaigrette

1 clove elephant garlic, peeled

1 sprig fresh thyme, stemmed and chopped

2 tablespoons olive oil

2 tablespoons white wine vinegar

Salt and pepper

1. Steam or boil the garlic until soft, then mash with the flat side of a knife until smooth.

2. In a small bowl, combine the mashed garlic with the thyme, olive oil, and vinegar. Stir together and season with salt and pepper. Set aside.

Salad

1½ cups fresh chanterelles or other wild mushrooms (such as oysters, shiitakes, portobellos)

1 tablespoon olive oil

1 shallot, peeled and chopped

½ teaspoon salt

¼ teaspoon black pepper

¾ cup French green beans or green beans, stem ends discarded

1 red or white endive, cored, rinsed, and separated into spears

1 small head frisée or chicory, cored, rinsed, and torn into large pieces

1. Fill a bowl with ice water.

2. Clean the mushrooms with a damp towel or brush.

3. In a small sauté pan over high heat, heat the oil until very hot. Add the mushrooms and shallot and sauté until the mushrooms are lightly browned, approximately 4 minutes. Season with salt and pepper.

4. In a small pot of lightly salted water, boil the beans for 5 minutes. Strain and cool in the ice bath.

5. In a large bowl, combine the mushrooms, endive, frisée or chicory, and green beans. Toss with the vinaigrette and serve.

Serves 2

Orecchiette Salad

Orecchiette, which means "small ears" in Italian, is an excellent pasta to use in chilled salads because its cup-like shape holds the dressing. Of course, you can use any other pasta that you have on hand and it will taste just as good.

Dressing

½ small red onion, peeled and finely chopped (about 1 cup)

¼ cup olive oil

3 tablespoons balsamic vinegar

¼ cup honey

1 teaspoon salt

1 teaspoon black pepper

1. In a small sauté pan over high heat, sauté the onion in the oil until golden brown, about 3–4 minutes.

2. Remove from the heat, add the vinegar and honey, and pour into a small container. Salt and pepper to taste. Set aside.

1. Fill a bowl with ice water.

2. In a large pot, bring 6 cups of lightly salted water to a boil. Add the asparagus and cook for 2 minutes. Remove the asparagus with a slotted spoon and cool in the ice bath. Pat dry and set aside.

3. Add the pasta to the boiling water and cook for approximately 14 minutes or until soft, stirring occasionally. Drain and cool in the ice bath. Let the pasta rest in a strainer for 5 minutes, then place it in a large bowl. Toss with a tablespoon of the olive oil and set aside.

4. Heat a large sauté pan over high heat. When the pan is very hot, add the remaining olive oil. When the oil starts to smoke, immediately add the mushrooms. Sauté, stirring occasionally, until the mushrooms are golden brown, about 5–6 minutes. Arrange the mushrooms (in a single layer, if possible) on a cookie sheet, and cool for 5 minutes.

5. Combine the pasta with the asparagus, mushrooms, spinach, and tomatoes. Carefully toss with half the vinaigrette and serve. (Any remaining vinaigrette will last several days tightly covered in the fridge.)

Serves 6

DANIEL'S TIP:
Do you know how to cut asparagus? Cut off and discard all the woody (and inedible) stems—about 2 inches from the bottom. Then cut the remaining asparagus on the diagonal into even-size tips and spears. Not only will your finished dish look better, but the asparagus will cook evenly.

Pasta

1 bunch asparagus, cut diagonally into tips and stems, woody bottoms discarded (see Daniel's Tip)

3 cups dried orecchiette pasta

2 tablespoons olive oil, divided

5 shiitake mushroom caps, cleaned and sliced, stems removed

3 portobello mushroom caps, cleaned and sliced

¾ cup oyster (or other available exotic) mushrooms, cleaned and sliced

2 cups chopped baby spinach leaves, stemmed, washed, and spun dry

15 cherry tomatoes, stemmed, washed, and cut in half

Panzanella

This is the quintessential summer salad, especially good when tomatoes are at their peak ripeness. I like to serve it as soon as it is tossed, with the baguettes straight out of the oven. The hot bread warms the other ingredients and accentuates their wonderful flavors.

4 medium-sized fresh native tomatoes, cored and cut into cubes

1 small baguette

¾ cup tightly packed fresh basil, washed

¼ cup olive oil

Juice and zest of 1 lemon

½ teaspoon cumin

1 clove garlic, peeled and chopped

1 cup pine nuts, lightly toasted, divided

¾ teaspoon salt

½ teaspoon black pepper

1. Preheat the oven to 350°F.

2. Place the tomatoes in a large bowl.

3. Cut the baguette into large cubes, place them on a cookie sheet, and lightly toast in the oven for about 10 minutes.

4. Puree the basil, olive oil, lemon juice, lemon zest, cumin, chopped garlic, and ½ cup of the pine nuts in a blender or food processor.

5. Add the warm bread, pureed basil pesto, and remaining ½ cup of pine nuts to the tomatoes. Season with salt and pepper. Toss and serve immediately.

Serves 4

DANIEL'S TIP:
If you core a lot of tomatoes, consider spending a few dollars on a tomato huller. They're cheap, effective, and do double duty hulling strawberries. This is one of those gadgets in your kitchen gadget drawer that you will actually use.

Wild Mushroom, Apple, and Smoked Pecan Salad with Melted Red Onion and Bacon Dressing

In this fantastic autumn salad, the smokiness of the pecans combines with the earthiness of the mushrooms, the fruit of the apple, and the aromas of the dark beer and malt vinegar to create something memorable.

1. In a small sauté pan over medium-high heat, cook the bacon until crisp. Remove the bacon, drain on paper towels, and set aside.

2. Add the olive oil, onion, and mushrooms to the bacon fat, and cook, over medium-high heat, until the onion is very tender, about 8 minutes, stirring occasionally. Stir in the beer and vinegar. Bring to a boil, remove from the heat, season with salt and pepper, and allow to cool to room temperature.

3. In a large bowl, mix the lettuces with half the dressing, the sliced apples, and the reserved bacon. Adjust the salt and pepper as necessary and serve garnished with the pecans. (Any remaining dressing will last several days tightly covered in the refrigerator.)

Serves 4

Dressing

4 strips bacon, cut into small pieces
3 tablespoons olive oil
1 small red onion, peeled and finely chopped
1 cup assorted wild mushrooms, sliced
¼ cup dark beer
¼ cup malt vinegar
¾ teaspoon salt
½ teaspoon black pepper

4 cups mixed baby lettuces, packed
1 green apple, cored, peeled, and diced
½ cup smoked pecans (or smoked almonds), for garnish

Arugula, Yellow Bean, Asparagus, and Tomato Salad

It doesn't get more summery than this salad with its vibrant colors and fresh-from-the-garden vegetables and herbs. Best of all, it's so easy to make.

1 pound green asparagus

1 cup yellow wax or green beans

½ pint red cherry tomatoes, washed, stemmed, and cut in half

½ pint yellow cherry tomatoes, washed, stemmed, and cut in half

2 cups local baby arugula, packed

½ teaspoon salt

¼ teaspoon black pepper

3 tablespoons balsamic vinegar

3 tablespoons olive oil

2 tablespoons chopped fresh tarragon

½ cup grated Parmigiana Reggiano

1. Bring a large pot of salted water to a brisk boil. Fill a large bowl with ice water.

2. Cut off and discard the woody ends of the asparagus. Diagonally cut each spear in half. Cook the asparagus pieces in the boiling water until crunchy but tender, about 4–5 minutes. Remove the asparagus from the boiling water with a slotted spoon and place in the ice water.

3. Wash and snip off the ends of the beans. Cook the beans in the boiling water until fork-tender, about 6–8 minutes. Remove the beans from the boiling water and place with the asparagus in the ice water (replenishing the ice, if necessary).

4. Drain the asparagus and beans and pat dry with paper towels. Set aside.

5. In a large bowl, combine the asparagus, beans, tomatoes, and baby arugula. Generously sprinkle with salt and pepper. Toss with the balsamic vinegar, olive oil, and tarragon. Sprinkle with the grated cheese and serve.

Serves 4–6

Baby Herb Greens and Red Wine Vinaigrette

This very simple mixed-greens salad goes particularly well with red wines. Most salad dressings have very high acidity levels, which overpower the flavors of wine. Because the dressing of this salad is made with red wine, it complements an accompanying red wine.

2 shallots, peeled and thinly sliced
¾ teaspoon salt
¼ teaspoon black pepper
1 cup red wine (if possible, use the same wine you plan to drink with dinner, or something close)
3 tablespoons olive oil
2 tablespoons honey
6 cups herb salad mix or 1 (7-ounce) package baby greens
Toasted walnuts, for garnish (optional)

1. Place the shallots in a bowl, sprinkle with salt and pepper, and set aside.

2. In a small sauté pan, over medium heat, reduce the wine to ⅛ cup, about 15–20 minutes. Pour over the shallots. Stir in the olive oil and honey. Let the mixture come to room temperature.

3. Toss the greens in half the red wine dressing and serve, garnished with toasted walnuts. (Any remaining dressing will last for several days, tightly covered in the refrigerator.)

Serves 4

Shopping

My approach to grocery shopping is not unlike my approach to foraging; I look for what's fresh and in season and then cook dinner around what I've found.

I generally don't have an idea about what I'm going to serve that evening until I go to the store and look around. Especially the produce department. The vegetable and fruit selection can change so dramatically and so quickly—and I want to tap into the freshest available ingredients. If you're uncomfortable being so last-minute, at least go shopping with the idea that you may change some of your dishes that evening to reflect what you find. Be open to spontaneity; you'll taste the difference in your cooking.

And make friends with the men and women who work at your local market. I now know the butcher at my neighborhood store by name. He doesn't know I'm a chef but he will go out of his way to make sure I have the freshest meats. And he always has a special cut in the back he thinks I might want to try. It's not quite like the days when dinner was whatever my dad had hunted that afternoon—but it's not all that different, either.

Caponata

This dish may have originated in the Mediterranean, but with all the wonderful vegetables available at your local farm stand or markets, you can enjoy it year-round. This salad can also be served hot as a side dish with red meat, especially lamb. Remember to keep the pan on high heat when you're sautéing all the vegetables.

1. Cut the eggplant, tomatoes, onion, zucchini, and summer squash into small cubes approximately ½ inch, keeping each vegetable separate.

2. Heat 6 tablespoons of the olive oil in a large sauté pan over high heat. When the oil starts to smoke, add the eggplant and sauté until light brown on all sides, about 4 minutes. Stir in the tomatoes, toss for 30 seconds, then remove the vegetables from the pan and allow to cool on a cookie sheet.

3. Add the remaining 2 tablespoons of olive oil to the sauté pan. When it starts to smoke, add the onion and sauté for 2 minutes. Add the zucchini and summer squash and cook for an additional 4 minutes, stirring occasionally. Add the olives, cook for an additional minute, and remove the pan from the heat. Combine with the rest of the vegetables on the cookie sheet.

4. When the vegetables are cool, transfer to a bowl. Season with the salt and pepper and stir in the chopped basil.

Serves 8

1 medium-sized eggplant, stemmed
2 plum or vine-ripened tomatoes, cored
1 medium-sized red onion, peeled
1 small zucchini, stemmed
1 small summer squash, stemmed
½ cup olive oil, divided
1 cup pitted kalamata olives
¾ teaspoon salt
¼ teaspoon black pepper
½ cup chopped fresh basil

Beet and Goat Cheese "Autumn Sunset" Salad

I call this "Autumn Sunset" because it reminds me of the beautiful colors you can see on a crisp, clear fall evening in New England. Look for beets the size of small tennis balls.

Dressing

2 tablespoons apple cider

2 tablespoons cider vinegar

¼ cup olive oil

1 shallot, peeled and finely chopped

¾ teaspoon salt

½ teaspoon cracked black pepper

Place the apple cider, vinegar, olive oil, and shallot into a blender. Season with salt and pepper. Blend for 30 seconds, correct the seasoning if necessary, and set aside.

Salad

2 medium-sized yellow beets

2 medium-sized red beets

2 bunches watercress, washed and drained

½ cup soft goat cheese

1. In a large saucepan, cover the beets with several inches of lightly salted cold water. Bring to a boil, lower the heat, and simmer for approximately 45 minutes or until you can easily pierce the beets through the center with a toothpick.

2. Rinse the beets under cold water to cool. When the beets are at room temperature, peel them and cut them into ⅛-inch-thick slices.

3. Arrange the beets, alternating colors, in concentric circles on the outer edges of four salad plates. Place the watercress in the middle of each plate. Drizzle with the dressing and garnish with crumbled goat cheese.

Serves 4

DANIEL'S TIP:
Peel beets under water. It keeps the beet skins moist and pliant and makes peeling hassle-free.

Florence's Macaroni and Hard-Boiled Egg Salad

My first cooking job was at The Candlelight, a small family-run restaurant in Skowhegan, Maine, owned by Florence Blaisdell-Sterns. Florence was one of the hardest-working people I've ever met, and I am who I am today in large part because of her influence. Every Sunday brunch she made this simple yet tasty macaroni salad with its classic sprinkling of paprika.

1. Coarsely chop two of the eggs. Cut the remaining two eggs in half.

2. In a decorative serving bowl, combine the onion, celery, and bell pepper. Sprinkle with the salt and pepper and let sit for 10 minutes.

3. Add the chopped eggs, macaroni, mayonnaise, lemon juice, sage, and parsley. Toss together and top with the hard-boiled egg halves and a sprinkling of paprika.

Serves 4

DANIEL'S TIP:
For perfect hard-boiled eggs, start the eggs in cold, lightly salted water; the water should cover the eggs by ½ inch. Bring the water to a boil, lower the heat to a soft rolling boil, and cook for 6 minutes. Remove the eggs and immediately cool in an ice bath. Your eggs will never have the green edge that comes from cooking eggs too quickly at too high a temperature.

4 hard-boiled eggs, peeled and chilled
1 small red onion, peeled and finely chopped
1 celery stalk, finely chopped
1 small red bell pepper, stemmed, seeded, and finely chopped
¼ teaspoon salt
¼ teaspoon black pepper
2 cups cooked elbow macaroni
¼ cup mayonnaise
Juice of 1 lemon
½ teaspoon dry sage or 2 leaves fresh sage, chopped
1 tablespoon chopped fresh parsley
½ teaspoon paprika

Caramelized Pear, Roquefort, and Candied Walnut Salad

Roquefort, a pungent blue cheese, may not be for everyone, but when the saltiness of the cheese combines with the sweetness of pears and nutty walnuts, it takes on an entirely different taste profile.

Dressing

¼ cup cider vinegar
1 shallot, peeled
1 teaspoon honey
½ cup olive oil
½ teaspoon salt
¼ teaspoon black pepper

Place the vinegar, shallot, honey, and olive oil in a blender. Season with salt and pepper. Blend for 30 seconds. Scrape into a container and set aside.

Salad

¾ cup shelled walnut halves
1 egg white
1 tablespoon sugar
1 firm Bartlett pear (or any other firm pear)
1 tablespoon olive oil
1 head frisée or chicory, stemmed, washed, and torn into large pieces; or 1 (7-ounce) bag mixed greens of your choice
4 ounces roquefort cheese (or your favorite pungent blue cheese), crumbled

1. Preheat the oven to 350°F.

2. In small bowl, toss the walnuts with the egg white and sugar. Arrange the walnuts on a cookie sheet lined with waxed paper that's been lightly sprayed with oil. Bake for 15 minutes and allow to cool.

3. Core the pear, cut it in half, and then cut each half into six even wedges (to make twelve wedges total).

4. Heat the olive oil in a medium-sized sauté pan over medium heat. Add the pears and cook until golden brown and caramelized, about 6–7 minutes per side. Remove from the heat and allow to cool.

5. In a bowl, toss the greens with the dressing to taste. Arrange the greens in the centers of four plates. Top with the walnuts, three wedges of pear per plate, and the crumbled roquefort. (Any remaining dressing will last several days tightly covered in the refrigerator.)

Serves 4

DANIEL'S TIP:
Looking for a quick snack? The walnuts-baked-in-egg-white-and-sugar step of this recipe works just as well with any nut—try almonds, peanuts, or cashews.

Tossed Hearts of Romaine with Melted Cheddar Cheese and Spinach Toast

This alternative to a Caesar salad uses crispy hearts of romaine. Because the cheese and spinach toasts go like hotcakes, I've doubled the recipe—everyone always clamors for more.

Dressing

1 egg yolk

1 clove garlic, peeled and finely chopped

Juice of 1 lemon

3 tablespoons Dijon mustard

1 tablespoon water

½ teaspoon salt

1 teaspoon cracked black pepper

½ cup olive oil

In a bowl, whisk together the egg yolk, garlic, lemon juice, mustard, water, salt, and pepper. When thoroughly combined, whisk in the olive oil. Set aside.

Salad

1 large baguette

3 tablespoons olive oil

1½ cups grated cheddar cheese

1½ cups finely chopped spinach

2 hearts of romaine, roughly chopped

1. Preheat the oven to 425°F.

2. Thinly slice the baguette on a wide angle to create long slices, about ⅛ inch thick, yielding approximately 18 slices. Arrange the slices on a cookie sheet. Drizzle with the olive oil.

3. In a bowl, mix together the cheddar and chopped spinach. Mound the cheese-and-spinach mixture on the tops of the baguette slices. Bake for 10–12 minutes or until bubbling.

4. Meanwhile, in a bowl, toss the romaine with dressing to taste. Divide the salad onto four plates and top each plate with two of the cheese-and-spinach toasts. Pass the remaining toasts. (Any remaining dressing will last several days tightly covered in the refrigerator.)

Serves 4

Chopped Salad with Aged Sherry and Buttermilk Dressing

Chopped salads are a nice way to use up any fresh ingredients in your refrigerator because they can be made with so many different ingredients—from meats to cheeses and vegetables.

Place the vinegar, buttermilk, olive oil, honey, salt, and pepper in a blender. Blend for 30 seconds. Set aside.

1. In a large bowl, toss the lettuce with dressing to taste.

2. Divide the lettuce onto four plates. Top with the bacon, tomatoes, cucumber, scallions, chickpeas, and olives. Serve. (Any remaining dressing will last several days tightly covered in the refrigerator.)

Serves 4

Dressing

1½ tablespoons aged sherry vinegar

3 tablespoons buttermilk

½ cup olive oil

1 tablespoon honey

½ teaspoon salt

¼ teaspoon black pepper

Salad

1 head iceberg lettuce, cored and chopped into 2-inch pieces

4 slices crisp bacon, chopped

2 plum tomatoes, cored and chopped

1 English cucumber, chopped

1 bunch scallions, ends discarded and finely chopped

½ cup chickpeas

½ cup pitted olives

Rowes Wharf Crab, Tomato, and Avocado Salad with Horseradish Dressing

I've been making this salad since 1989 when I first became chef at the Boston Harbor Hotel—and it's never left the menu. I wanted to create a signature salad and, since the hotel is located on the water, crabmeat seemed a natural fit.

Dressing

1 egg yolk

1 tablespoon jarred white
   horseradish

2 tablespoons whole-milk
   yogurt

Juice of 1 lemon

1 clove garlic, peeled

3 tablespoons water

½ teaspoon salt

¼ teaspoon white pepper

⅓ cup olive oil

1. Place the egg yolk, horseradish, yogurt, lemon juice, garlic, and water in a blender. Season with salt and pepper.

2. Turn the blender on and slowly add the olive oil. Scrape the dressing into a small container and set aside.

Salad

1 ripe avocado

1 medium-sized red tomato,
   washed, cored, and cut
   into 4 slices

1 medium-sized yellow
   tomato, washed, cored,
   and cut into 4 slices

2 tablespoons capers,
   drained

1 head hydroponic Bibb
   lettuce, torn into large
   pieces

½ pound fresh local (or best-
   quality) crabmeat (in New
   England we like Jonah or
   peekytoe)

1. Peel the avocado, remove the pit, and cut into eight slices.

2. Place one red and one yellow slice of tomato on the side of a salad plate. Top each tomato slice with a slice of avocado and sprinkle with capers.

3. Toss the lettuce with dressing to taste and arrange next to the tomatoes. Top with the crabmeat and serve. (Any remaining dressing will last tightly covered in the refrigerator for several days.)

Serves 4

DANIEL'S TIP:
When selecting avocados, look for those whose skin has lightly darkened. When pressing with your thumb, you should feel a slight give. Too firm means the avocado won't be flavorful; too much give means the flesh will be dark when you slice the avocado open.

FISH

As the son of a registered Maine guide, I grew up fishing. Because I've spent the past twenty-five years working on Boston Harbor, fish is one of the ingredients I most enjoy working with. Fish must be perfectly fresh, and you need a delicate and deft hand to highlight its flavors.

Baked Flounder with Potatoes and Leeks

To my mind, there's no more Down East Maine dish than this. Flounder is a delicate and flavorful fish that doesn't need much cooking. That translates into a quick and delicious dinner.

6 tablespoons (¾ stick) butter, divided

2 medium-sized Maine (or your favorite) potatoes, about ¾ pound total, peeled and diced

1 leek, white and light green parts, cut into ⅛-inch-thick rounds and thoroughly washed

1 teaspoon salt, divided

¼ teaspoon white pepper

1 clove garlic, peeled and chopped

1 cup panko bread crumbs

¼ cup washed and chopped parsley

4 flounder fillets (4–6 ounces each), center bone removed

Juice of 1 lemon

1. Preheat the oven to 375°F.

2. In a heavy-bottomed sauté pan over medium heat, melt 3 tablespoons of the butter. When the butter starts to bubble, add the potatoes and leeks to the pan. Toss to coat with melted butter, cover, and cook for 12 minutes, stirring occasionally, until the vegetables are tender. Season with ¾ teaspoon of the salt and the white pepper. Pour into the bottom of an 8 x 8-inch ovenproof casserole.

3. In a second sauté pan over medium heat, melt the remaining 3 tablespoons of butter with the chopped garlic. When the butter starts to bubble, add the bread crumbs, parsley, and the remaining ¼ teaspoon of salt. Toss together until the crumbs are lightly browned.

4. Arrange the flounder fillets, white-side up, over the potatoes and leeks, leaving a small gap between the fillets. Drizzle lemon juice over the fish, sprinkle with the bread crumbs, and bake for 12–14 minutes or until the fish is done.

Serves 4

Baked North Atlantic Halibut with Wild Mushroom Crust

This dish combines the largest flatfish in the world (halibut can weigh over seven hundred pounds) with my favorite wild mushrooms.

3 tablespoons butter

2 tablespoons peeled and chopped shallots

1 teaspoon peeled and chopped garlic

2 cups assorted wild mushrooms, thinly sliced

½ cup bread crumbs

1 tablespoon heavy cream

1 egg, beaten

1½ teaspoons salt, divided

½ teaspoon white pepper, divided

4 (5-ounce) skinless Atlantic halibut fillets

1½ tablespoons olive oil

1. Preheat the oven to 400°F.

2. Heat a medium-sized sauté pan over high heat. Add the butter, shallots, garlic, and mushrooms; sauté for approximately 4 minutes, being careful not to overstir, until the mushrooms are browned.

3. Transfer the mushrooms to a bowl and cool for 5 minutes. Stir in the bread crumbs, cream, and beaten egg. Season with ½ teaspoon of the salt and ¼ teaspoon of the pepper.

4. Rub the halibut fillets with the oil and sprinkle with the remaining 1 teaspoon salt and ¼ teaspoon pepper. Arrange them on a lightly oiled roasting pan. Cover the top of each fillet evenly with the mushroom mixture.

5. Roast for 10 minutes or until the halibut juices begin to congeal on the surface.

Serves 4

Winter Cod with Chorizo, Red Peppers, and White Beans

Cod is best during winter months because the texture tends to be firmer due to the cold water. This recipe salutes the Portuguese community of southeastern Massachusetts.

1. Lightly salt both sides of the cod fillets, arrange on a plate, and refrigerate for 1 hour.

2. Preheat the oven to 350°F.

3. In a nonstick sauté pan over medium-high heat, heat the oil to the smoking point.

4. Add the cod fillets, flesh-side down, and quickly sauté on both sides until golden brown, about 4 minutes a side. Remove the fillets to a cookie sheet covered with waxed paper or oil.

5. In the same pan over medium heat, sauté the peppers until they're tender, about 5 minutes. Season with salt and pepper.

6. Add the greens and sauté until wilted, about 3 minutes.

7. Add the chorizo, beans, basil, and water and cook until thoroughly heated. Add additional salt and pepper if necessary.

8. Meanwhile, place the cod in an ovenproof dish and bake for 5 minutes or until the flesh is opaque but still moist.

9. Divide the pepper-and-bean mixture among six plates and top with the cod.

Serves 6

6 (5-ounce) cod fillets
2 teaspoons coarse salt
3 tablespoons olive oil
2 red bell peppers, stemmed, seeded, and sliced into rings
Pepper, to taste
1 pound winter greens (collard, swiss chard, or kale), stemmed, washed, and chopped
½ pound chorizo, thinly sliced
1 cup cooked great northern white beans
6 basil leaves, slivered
3 tablespoons water

DANIEL'S TIP:
If you lightly sprinkle coarse salt over both sides of lean, flaky fish fillets like cod, haddock, hake, and pollack and refrigerate them an hour before cooking, the salt "cures" the flesh and prevents the fillets from flaking while cooking.

Pan-Fried Crispy Trout

When I was young, I spent hours stomping up and down small mountain streams in New Hampshire and Maine in search of brook trout. I'd take them home, dredge them in cornmeal and flour, and fry them up. It's still my favorite way to prepare trout.

4 (8–10 ounce) head-off, bone-in brook or rainbow trout
½ cup buttermilk
½ cup all-purpose flour
½ cup cornmeal
1 teaspoon salt
½ teaspoon white pepper
2½ tablespoons butter
2½ tablespoons olive oil

1. In a large bowl, soak the trout in the buttermilk for 5 minutes.

2. Sift the flour, cornmeal, salt, and pepper into a large zip-top bag.

3. In a large, preferably cast-iron frying pan, melt the butter and oil over medium-high heat.

4. When the oil begins to smoke, place the trout in the plastic bag with the flour-and-cornmeal mixture and gently shake. Remove the trout from the bag, gently shaking again to remove any excess flour, and place in the frying pan.

5. Fry the trout until crisp on both sides, approximately 6–7 minutes per side. Serve immediately.

Serves 4

DANIEL'S TIP:
Using a plastic zip-top bag to dredge fish (or poultry or meat) is a great method to ensure that your fish is evenly coated in flour. When you're done, simply discard the bag; there's no extra bowl to wash.

Balsamic and Basil Glazed Grilled Atlantic Mackerel with Sweet Corn, Pea, and Tomato Salad

I used to drive down to the Cape Cod Canal, cast my rigs out into the tidal stream, and pull in three or four mackerel at a time. These beautiful, streamlined fish with their iridescent colors are spectacular to behold. Because of their high oil content, which becomes overpowering over time, mackerel should be cooked and eaten right out of the water whenever possible. It is a perfect fish for the grill.

Glaze

2 cups balsamic vinegar

8 basil leaves

In small saucepot over medium-high heat, reduce the vinegar and basil to ¼ cup. Remove the basil leaves from the glaze and discard. Set aside.

Sweet Corn, Pea, and Tomato Salad

2 ears sweet corn

½ cup English peas

½ cup snap peas

½ cup arugula

½ cup red and yellow cherry tomatoes, cut in halves

3–4 basil leaves, slivered

½ teaspoon salt

½ teaspoon cracked black pepper

2 tablespoons olive oil

2 tablespoons balsamic vinegar

1. Remove the kernels from the ears of corn (see page 58). Fill a large bowl with ice water.

2. In a pot of boiling, lightly salted water, cook the corn kernels, English peas, and snap peas for 2 minutes.

3. Remove the vegetables from the pot and immediately plunge into the ice water. When the vegetables are chilled, drain and dry them and transfer to a bowl.

4. Add the arugula, cherry tomatoes, and slivered basil to the bowl. Season with salt and pepper and gently toss with the olive oil and balsamic. Divide the salad onto four plates.

Mackerel

4 (5-ounce) fresh mackerel fillets

½ teaspoon salt

½ teaspoon black pepper

1. Preheat a grill until it's very hot.

2. With a sharp knife, score the mackerel skin every ½ inch to form diagonal cuts and prevent curling. Season both sides of the fillets with salt and pepper and brush both sides with glaze.

3. Brush the grill with olive oil. Lay the mackerel fillets skin down on the grill and cook until the skin shows char marks, about 2 minutes. Turn the fish over, brush with more glaze, and grill another 4–5 minutes or until the flesh is cooked but not too dry.

4. Serve the mackerel on top of the corn, pea, and tomato salad with a drizzle of any remaining glaze.

Serves 4

Pan-Roasted Atlantic Swordfish Steaks in Riesling, Lemongrass, Ginger, Carrot, and Coconut Broth

Swordfish can weigh up to a thousand pounds. I prefer those weighing about 120 pounds, because the steaks are the perfect size. This dish is a shout-out to Boston's thriving Chinatown.

1. Cut the lemongrass stalk in half. Discard the upper part of the stalk and gently crush the lower part with the backside of a knife.

2. In a large saucepan, bring the lemongrass, ginger, Riesling, carrot juice, coconut milk, honey, chile paste, and ¼ teaspoon of the salt to a boil. Lower the heat and simmer for 20 minutes. Strain the broth and discard the solids.

3. Return the broth to the pan and bring to a simmer. Add the baby bok choy and cook until tender, about 5 minutes.

4. Heat a nonstick pan over high heat and add the olive oil. Sprinkle the swordfish steaks with the remaining ¾ teaspoon salt. When the oil starts to smoke, add the swordfish and sauté until it's golden brown, about 5 minutes per side.

5. Place the swordfish and baby bok choy into four bowls. Ladle the broth over the fish and bok choy and serve.

Serves 4

1 stalk lemongrass
1 (1-inch) piece fresh ginger, peeled and roughly chopped
½ cup Riesling (or other fruity white wine)
1 cup carrot juice
½ cup coconut milk
1 tablespoon honey
1 teaspoon chile paste
1 teaspoon salt, divided
4 baby bok choy, thoroughly washed
1 tablespoon olive oil
4 (5-ounce) swordfish steaks

Pan-Roasted Striped Bass with Orange Ale Essence

With beer more popular than ever before, I was approached by the *Boston Globe* to create dishes pairing different styles of beer. It was a different take on my lifelong passion for pairing wine and food. This striped bass was the result.

Sauce

1 cup orange juice
½ cup pale ale
4 tablespoons (½ stick) cold
   butter, cut into cubes
¼ teaspoon salt
Pinch of white pepper

1. In small saucepan, over medium-high heat, bring the orange juice and ale to a boil. Cook until the liquid reduces by half, stirring occasionally, about 3–4 minutes.

2. Turn down the heat to very low and whisk in the butter. Gently whisk until the butter is completely incorporated and the mixture has thickened. Season with salt and pepper and set aside, keeping warm.

Vegetables

3 ears fresh corn, shucked
1 leek
1 tablespoon butter
¼ teaspoon salt
Pinch of white pepper

1. Remove the corn kernels from the cobs (see page 58).

2. Slice the leek into thin rings, discarding the stem. Wash the rings thoroughly and pat dry.

3. Melt the butter in a sauté pan over medium heat. Add the leeks and sauté until tender, about 3–4 minutes, stirring occasionally. Add the corn and cook for an additional 2 minutes. Season with salt and pepper and set aside, keeping warm.

Fish

1 tablespoon olive oil
4 (5-ounce) striped bass
   fillets, skin on
¾ teaspoon salt
½ teaspoon white pepper
4 orange slices, peeled, for
   garnish
1 tablespoon minced fresh
   parsley, for garnish

1. Preheat the oven to 375°F.

2. In a large, ovenproof sauté pan, heat the olive oil to the smoking point over high heat.

3. Salt and pepper the bass fillets and add to the sauté pan, skin-side down. Pan-fry until the skin is golden brown, about 4–5 minutes.

4. Put the sauté pan with the fish into the oven and roast for 10 minutes.

5. Divide the sautéed corn and leeks among four dishes. Top with the striped bass and garnish with the orange ale essence, an orange slice, and a sprinkle of chopped parsley.

Serves 4

DANIEL'S TIP:
When making butter sauces, if the sauce is too warm, the butter will separate; if the sauce is too cool, it will congeal. Keep your sauce warm to the touch—if it feels too hot, remove it from your heat source.

Char-Grilled Grouper in Saffron Tomato Broth

Grouper is a firm fish, with the red and the black species being most readily available. The Provençal twist to this dish was inspired by my time working at Le Cirque in New York City alongside Chef Alain Sailhac, who's from southern France.

Broth

½ cup white wine

1 small onion, peeled and chopped

1 teaspoon saffron

6 plum tomatoes, cored and cut in half

3 cups fish stock (see page xxiv)

¾ teaspoon salt

¼ teaspoon white pepper

1. In a medium-sized saucepan, bring the white wine, onion, and saffron to a gentle boil. Simmer for 5 minutes.

2. Add the tomatoes and fish stock. Bring the mixture to a boil, reduce the heat, and simmer for an additional 15 minutes.

3. Strain the mixture through a strainer, pushing on the solids to extract all the flavorful juices. Season the broth with salt and pepper and set aside.

Saffron Rouille

2 tablespoons olive oil

2 cloves garlic, peeled

1 small onion, peeled and sliced

1 small potato, peeled and diced

2 tablespoons white wine

½ teaspoon saffron

1 plum tomato, cored and cut in quarters

2 tablespoons water

2 egg yolks

½ cup olive oil

½ teaspoon salt

¼ teaspoon white pepper

1. In a small saucepan, heat the olive oil over medium heat. Add the garlic, onion, and potato; sauté for 5 minutes, stirring often.

2. Add the white wine, saffron, tomato, and water. Bring to a boil, reduce the heat, cover tightly, and simmer over very low heat for 30 minutes or until the potato is very tender. Remove from the heat and cool to room temperature.

3. Place the mixture in the bowl of a food processor. Pulse the mixture off and on for 30 seconds. Add the egg yolks and, with the food processor running, drizzle in the olive oil. Season with salt and pepper.

1. Preheat a grill to hot.

2. Rub the fillets with oil and sprinkle with salt and pepper.

3. Grill the grouper, about 4–5 minutes per side, rotating each side diagonally during cooking to form cross marks.

4. Meanwhile, toast the baguette slices and top with the rouille.

5. Ladle the saffron broth into six bowls, place the fish in the broth, and finish with two slices of rouille-topped baguette.

Serves 6

Grouper

6 (5-ounce) grouper fillets (or any other firm white fish such as red snapper)
4 teaspoons olive oil
1½ teaspoons salt
½ teaspoon white pepper
12 slices French baguette

DANIEL'S TIP:
To prevent sticking on the grill, dip a paper towel or small dishtowel in salted oil and gently rub over the preheated grill before cooking.

Pan-Seared Salmon Paillards with Shiitake, Basil, Sweet Corn, and Watercress Sauté

A few years ago, I appeared with Ming Tsai on his PBS show *Simply Ming*, where I had to improvise a dish using mushrooms and basil. Even though it looks like it would take much longer, this seared salmon paillard dish can be prepared in less than 15 minutes—and you only need one pan.

Salmon

6 (5-ounce) skinless, boneless salmon fillets
3 tablespoons olive oil
1½ teaspoons salt
½ teaspoon white pepper

1. Butterfly the salmon fillets, place between plastic wrap on a cutting board, and gently pound with a meat mallet or the back of a flat-edged sharp knife to flatten the salmon into ¼-inch-thick paillards, being careful not to tear the fish.

2. Heat a large, nonstick sauté pan over high heat.

3. Rub the paillards with olive oil, season with salt and pepper, and immediately place in the hot pan.

4. In batches, sear the paillards until they're light golden brown, approximately 30 seconds, then flip over and cook for another 30–60 seconds, depending on how rare you like your salmon.

5. Place the salmon paillards on six plates. Reserve the sauté pan.

Shiitake, Basil, Sweet Corn, and Watercress Sauté

3 cups shiitake mushrooms
12 basil leaves
3 ears fresh corn
1 small lemon
3 tablespoons olive oil
4 cups watercress, stems removed
4 teaspoons capers
½ teaspoon salt
¼ teaspoon white pepper

1. Thinly slice the shiitake mushrooms. Thinly slice the basil. Cut the kernels from the ears of corn (see page 58). Grate or microplane the lemon and squeeze its juice. Combine the lemon zest and juice in a small bowl and discard the seeds.

2. Return the salmon sauté pan to the stove over high heat and add the olive oil.

3. When the oil starts to lightly smoke, immediately add the mushrooms and sauté for 1 minute or until the mushrooms start to brown.

4. Add the basil, corn kernels, watercress, and capers. Toss until the watercress is wilted, about 1 minute.

5. Add the lemon juice and zest, season with the salt and pepper, and spoon the vegetables over the center of each salmon paillard. Drizzle any remaining liquid around the salmon and serve.

Serves 6

Garlic-Marinated Shrimp Brochettes

These shrimp skewers are perfect for a casual dinner party or a lazy weekend around the house with family and friends. The combination of citrus, garlic, spices, and herbs make them very flavorful. The turmeric-soaked skewers add color—but the shrimp will taste just as good baked by themselves, minus the skewers.

1. In a large bowl, combine the chopped garlic, dill, chives, olive oil, lime zest and juice, salt, pepper, and optional Tabasco sauce. Add the shrimp, toss well, cover the bowl, and refrigerate for 2–3 hours, tossing once or twice.

2. If you're using wooden skewers, bring a small pot of water to a boil and add the turmeric. Pour the water over the skewers and soak for at least 1 hour. Metal skewers need not be soaked.

3. Preheat the oven to 450°F.

4. Arrange the shrimp (facing the same direction) on the six skewers.

5. Place the skewers on a lightly oiled rack on a cookie sheet. Bake for 8 minutes and serve.

Serves 6

2 cloves fresh garlic, peeled and chopped
2 tablespoons chopped fresh dill
2 tablespoons chopped fresh chives
¼ cup olive oil
Juice and zest of 1 lime
¼ teaspoon salt
¼ teaspoon cracked black pepper
¼ teaspoon Tabasco sauce (optional)
24 large (21–25 count per pound) shrimp, peeled and deveined, tails left on
6 skewers, preferably wooden
¼ teaspoon turmeric

New England Lobster and Clam Boil

I like to serve this summertime feast with grilled jumbo asparagus brushed with olive oil and sprinkled with coarse salt. The brilliant greens and flavor of the asparagus are perfect with this dish.

1. In a large (19-quart) lobster pot or its equivalent, combine the ale or beer, water, salt, lemon, tarragon, and butter. Bring to a boil over high heat.

2. Add the corn, lobsters, and clams. Cover and cook for 7 minutes.

3. Add the mussels, cover, and cook for another 3 minutes or until all the clams and mussels are open (discarding any clams and mussels that refuse to open).

4. Divide the shellfish and corn among four deep bowls and serve with cups of the broth, for dunking or drinking.

Serves 4

1 bottle Samuel Adams Summer Ale or Harpoon Summer Beer (or a good pilsner)
2 cups water
1½ teaspoons salt
1 lemon, cut in half
1 small bunch fresh tarragon
1 tablespoon butter
4 ears corn, shucked
4 (1–1½ pound) Maine lobsters
20 littlenecks or other hard-shell clams, washed
1 pound mussels, debearded

Sea Grille Tuna Niçoise

This recipe looks more complicated than it is. If you do it in steps, it can be on the table in 45 minutes. The key to this salad is the tuna. It must be pristinely fresh. If you're tight with your fishmonger, you ideally want a piece of center-cut tuna loin, trimmed into a 2-inch by 2-inch log, but a thick-as-possible tuna steak will do. And it's essential that your pan be smoking hot. You want to sear the rub until it's almost crunchy. Open all your windows and turn on the kitchen fan!

Potatoes, String Beans, and Eggs

4 Maine new potatoes or other small, thin-skinned potatoes

1 cup haricots verts or thin green string beans

2 eggs

1. Bring a large pot of salted water to a brisk boil. Fill a large bowl with ice water.

2. Cut the potatoes into quarters, drop them into the boiling water, and cook until fork-tender, about 10 minutes. Remove the potatoes with a slotted spoon, pat dry with paper towels, and immediately refrigerate.

3. Snip the ends off the haricots verts or string beans. Drop into the boiling water and cook for 1 minute (for the haricots verts) or 2–3 minutes (for the string beans). Remove the beans from the pot and plunge into the ice water. When they're cold, pat them dry with paper towels and let them join the potatoes in the refrigerator.

4. Lower the heat and bring the water to a simmer. Add the eggs and cook for 7 minutes. Remove from the water and cool. Peel and cut into quarters.

Dressing

3 tablespoons extra-virgin olive oil

3 tablespoons aged sherry vinegar

1 small shallot, finely chopped

¾ teaspoon salt

½ teaspoon black pepper

In a small bowl, whisk together the olive oil, sherry vinegar, and chopped shallot. Season with salt and pepper. Set aside.

Tuna

1 teaspoon Chinese five-
  spice powder
1 teaspoon brown sugar
1 teaspoon salt
1 teaspoon cracked black
  pepper
1 pound sushi-grade tuna
  (see headnote)
2 tablespoons olive oil

1. In a small bowl, combine the Chinese five-spice powder, brown sugar, teaspoon of salt, and teaspoon of pepper.

2. Rub the spice mix thoroughly into all sides of the tuna.

3. In a heavy-bottomed nonstick sauté pan or well-seasoned, cast-iron skillet, heat the olive oil over high heat. When the oil begins to smoke, add the tuna and sear on all sides until dark brown, 2–3 minutes per side depending on how rare you like it. Remove the tuna to a plate and set aside.

Assembly

2 cups frisée or your favorite
  baby greens
½ cup cherry tomatoes, cut
  in half
½ cup kalamata olives (or
  other black olives), pitted

1. In a large bowl, toss the frisée, cherry tomatoes, precooked potatoes, and precooked haricots verts with the dressing. Divide onto four plates.

2. Cut the tuna into thin slices and arrange over the tossed vegetables.

3. Garnish each plate with kalamata olives and precooked hard-boiled egg quarters. Serve immediately.

Serves 4

Le Cirque

When I returned to the United States after a two-year post-graduation stay in Europe, where I worked for one of Italy's most cutting-edge chefs, I applied for a job at Le Cirque. My Italian mentor Angelo Paracucchi knew the owner, Sirio Maccioni. I interviewed with Alain Sailhac, Le Cirque's famous French chef, but he didn't seem interested.

I was staying with friends in New Jersey and when I got home, they told me Sailhac had called. I called him back and said, "I got a message that you called," and he said, "I don't think so," and I said, "Okay, no problem," and went to hang up the phone. It was one of those defining moments in a career. I was taking the receiver off my ear when I heard him say, "Wait," and I said, "Yes?" He said, "How much money do you have to make?"

Now, you have to understand that the most money I'd ever made to that point was $120 a week. But I'd talked to a Johnson & Wales buddy who was pulling in sixty-something thousand being a chef, five years after graduation. So at that moment on the phone I didn't know what to say, but I had an idea that it would be nice to make $400 a week. So I said, "Four hundred dollars," and he said, "Gross or take-home?" And I said, "Gross, of course," and he said, "Can you start tomorrow morning at seven?" I said, "I'll be there."

I was assigned to the lunch fish station as the *poissonnier*—I had to get all the fish ready, the garnishes ready, and work the grill. It was a tough job, a monster job. I was working under a guy named James Bergin. And after three days, he said, "I'm outta here. I told the chef I wouldn't leave until we found a replacement. We tried a couple of people but you're the first one who can do it." I was pumped. "By the way," Bergin said, "how much are they paying you?" "Four hundred dollars," I said. He said, "That's not bad, I've been here three years and I'm making $475." I said, "How much is that take-home?" And he said, "That is take-home."

POULTRY

Wasn't it the Herbert Hoover campaign that promised "a chicken in every pot"? Americans love their chicken—and their turkey and, increasingly, their duck. Whether it's Super Bowl fried wings or the Thanksgiving turkey, we are a poultry nation.

S's "Fall Off the Bone" Crockpot Chicken

My ninety-three-year-old grandmother still cooks every day. When I was growing up, she made everything—from jams and preserves to pickles, baked goods, and elderberry wine. Everything was made with love. I remember walking into the kitchen, sitting at the table, and tasting this chicken for the first time. I couldn't believe how tender it was. It is still my favorite chicken to eat.

1 (3-pound) fryer chicken

5 cups water

4 teaspoons salt

1 teaspoon black pepper

1 onion, peeled and cut in quarters

2 celery stalks, trimmed and cut into 2-inch sections

2 carrots, peeled and cut into 2-inch sections

2 potatoes, peeled and cut in quarters

1 cup button mushrooms, washed

1. Place the chicken, breast-side down, in the crockpot, along with the water, salt, and pepper. Cook on high setting for 3½ hours.

2. Add the onion, celery, carrots, potatoes, and mushrooms. Turn the crockpot to low and cook for another 2½ hours. Serve.

Serves 4

NANA'S TIP:
My grandmother's secret ingredient is half a package of dried onion soup, which she adds with the water. She swears by it. Being a "from-scratch" guy, I didn't include it in the list of ingredients, but I do love her chicken.

Dried Cranberry and Spinach Stuffed Chicken Breast

This recipe looks more difficult to make than it actually is. Believe me, you'll love the results, and you can prepare it in advance through the frying. Pop the fried chicken rolls in the oven when your guests arrive. Just to forewarn you, when you make this dish, you're going to end up with half an unused chicken breast. Sauté it later to put into a sandwich or on top of a salad.

4 (7-ounce) boneless,
  skinless chicken breasts
1¼ teaspoons salt, divided
½ teaspoon white pepper
1 packed cup spinach,
  washed and chopped
½ cup heavy cream
½ cup dried cranberries
⅓ cup all-purpose flour,
  sifted
1 egg
2 cups panko bread crumbs
⅔ cup olive oil

1. Preheat the oven to 375°F.

2. Lay three of the chicken breasts on a clean work surface. Using a sharp knife, cut each breast, horizontally left to right, up to—but not through—the right side, so that you can open the breast up like a book. Slightly pound with a wooden mallet or the side of a cleaver so that the thickness of the meat is even and the breast is rectangular in shape.

3. Cut half of the remaining chicken breast into large cubes. Reserve the remaining breast half for another purpose (see headnote).

4. Place the chicken cubes into the bowl of a food processor with 1 teaspoon of the salt and the ½ teaspoon white pepper. Pulse until lightly ground. Add the spinach and heavy cream and pulse again until the cream is fully incorporated, about 20 seconds.

5. Transfer the mixture to a small bowl and fold in the cranberries.

6. Lay a row of the spinach filling down the center of each pounded chicken breast. Roll each breast to form a log.

7. Place the flour in a shallow bowl with the remaining ¼ teaspoon salt. In a second bowl, beat the egg. Place the panko in a shallow, lipped pan.

8. Dredge the chicken rolls in the flour, then the egg, and finally the bread crumbs, making sure to coat them evenly on all sides.

9. Heat the olive oil in a large frying pan over medium-high heat. Just before the oil begins to smoke, carefully place the chicken breasts in the pan. Fry the rolls on each side, approximately 1 minute per side, until the entire roll is golden brown.

10. Remove the rolls to a rack in a roasting pan and roast for 24 minutes. Rest for 5 minutes, then slice and serve.

Serves 6

Maple and Chile Glazed Chicken Breasts

This chicken is insanely easy to make and crazy good. Everyone loves the hot and sweet marinade, which slightly brines the chicken, infusing it with flavor. If you grill the chicken, you only want to mark the surface—otherwise the sugar in the marinade will burn. You then finish the dish off in the oven. If you don't have a grill, pan-sear the chicken in a nonstick sauté pan before it goes in the oven.

1. In a large bowl, toss the onion with the salt. Let rest for 15 minutes. Add the maple syrup and red chile paste to the onion and its juices and mix well.

2. Add the chicken breasts, coat with the marinade, and refrigerate for at least 1 hour and up to 3 hours.

3. Preheat a grill to high and the oven to 400°F.

4. Sear the chicken on the grill for 1–2 minutes a side to mark the skin (alternatively, pan-sear it in a nonstick sauté pan over medium heat on the stove). Transfer the chicken to a lightly oiled baking dish and roast in the oven, skin-side up, for 20 minutes.

Serves 4

1 medium-sized red onion, peeled and thinly sliced
1 teaspoon salt
¼ cup maple syrup
1 tablespoon red chile paste or sambal
4 boneless chicken breast halves, skin on or off, approximately ½ pound each

DANIEL'S TIP:
When preparing marinades or salsas, salt your onions for 15 minutes before adding any other ingredients. The salting softens the pungency of the onions and makes for more balanced flavors. Try it next time you make guacamole.

Kale Stuffed Roast Turkey Breast

Turkey isn't just for Thanksgiving anymore. Ask your butcher to butterfly the turkey breast and pound it ¾ inch thick. Or follow my instructions and do it yourself with a sharp knife and wooden mallet.

¼ cup pearl barley

2½ teaspoons salt, divided

1½ teaspoons white pepper, divided

4 tablespoons (½ stick) butter, divided

1 tablespoon chopped fresh sage

2 teaspoons chopped garlic

1 pound kale, stems discarded, leaves washed and roughly chopped

1 (2½–3 pound) boneless turkey breast

1. Preheat the oven to 400°F.

2. Rinse the barley in cold water and drain. In a medium-sized saucepan over high heat, pour the barley into 2 cups boiling water. Lower the heat and simmer until the barley is fully cooked, about 30 minutes. Drain, season with ¼ teaspoon of the salt and ¼ teaspoon of the white pepper. Set aside.

3. In a large sauté pan, melt 2 tablespoons of the butter over medium heat. Add the sage, garlic, and kale; sauté until the kale is wilted, about 5 minutes. Remove from the heat, drain off any liquid, and place in a small bowl. Toss with ¼ teaspoon salt and ¼ teaspoon white pepper and cool.

4. To butterfly the turkey breast, remove the skin and lay the breast on a clean work surface with the tip of the breast facing you. Using a sharp knife, cut the breast, left to right, up to, but not through, the right side, so that you can open the breast up like a book. You'll get a rectangular piece of meat. Lightly pound the breast with a wooden mallet or the side of a cleaver so that it's ¾ inch thick.

5. Sprinkle the pounded turkey breast with 1 teaspoon salt and ½ teaspoon white pepper. Spread an even layer of kale over the surface of the turkey. Make a 2-inch-wide row of barley, lengthwise down the middle of the kale.

6. Roll the turkey, lengthwise, into a sausage-shaped package and tie, end-to-end, with kitchen twine. Melt the remaining 2 tablespoons of butter in the sauté pan over medium heat and rub over the entire turkey, top and bottom. Likewise, sprinkle the remaining 1 teaspoon of salt and ½ teaspoon of white pepper over the entire turkey.

7. Place the turkey on a rack in a roasting pan. Fill the pan with 1 inch of water, making sure it doesn't touch the rack.

8. Roast the turkey breast for 65–70 minutes or until a thermometer inserted into the center registers 165°F.

9. Let the turkey rest for 10 minutes before carving.

Serves 6–8

Lemon and Thyme Roasted Chicken

A perfectly roasted chicken is simple to prepare. There are so few steps, everything hinges on it being cooked and seasoned properly. In this flavorful recipe, the smell of lemon, garlic, and roasting chicken will make your mouth water.

1 head garlic
2 tablespoons olive oil
1 teaspoon salt
½ teaspoon white pepper
2 sprigs fresh thyme
1 (3–3½ pound) roaster chicken
1 small lemon, cut in half

1. Preheat the oven to 400°F.

2. Cut the head of garlic in half, horizontally, to expose all the cloves.

3. In a small bowl, mix together the olive oil, salt, pepper, and thyme. Rub the cavity of the chicken with half the mixture. Then place the garlic and lemon halves in the cavity of the chicken as well.

4. Truss the chicken (see Daniel's Tip), then rub the outside with the remaining seasoned olive oil. Place on a rack in a roasting pan, breast-side up. Add ½ inch water to the roasting pan, making sure it doesn't touch the rack.

5. Roast the chicken for 30 minutes. Reduce the oven temperature to 375°F and continue roasting for another 30 minutes. Turn off the oven and allow the chicken to remain in the oven an additional 15 minutes. Remove the chicken from the oven, cut off the trussing string, carve, and serve.

Serves 3–4

DANIEL'S TIP:

Trussing a chicken creates a beautifully shaped bird that is easy to carve. Try it: Lay the chicken on a work surface breast-side up, with wings pointing at you. Cut an 18-inch length of butcher's twine (available in all supermarkets). Place the center of the twine under the tail, then lift—and cross—the ends of the string to form a loop around the legs of the chicken. Pull tightly on both ends of the butcher's twine so that the legs come together. Then, pull the ends of the twine toward the front end of the chicken. Keeping it tight, tie the twine around the neck end of the chicken. Cut off and discard any extra string.

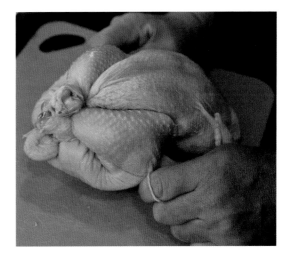

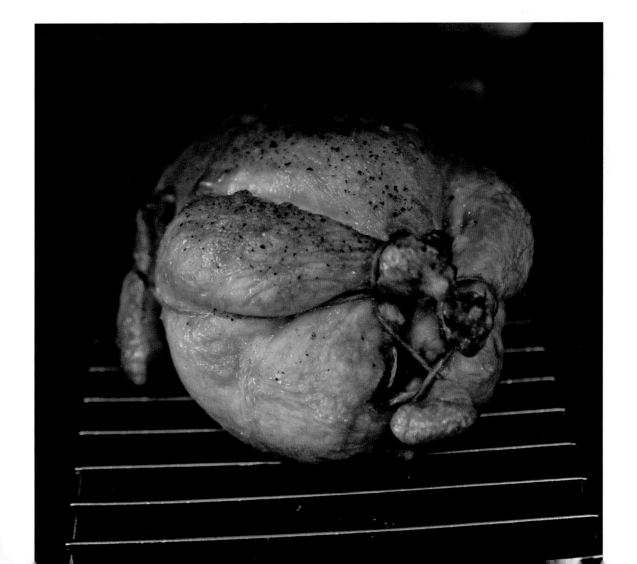

Molasses Barbecued Chicken

Ever since the rum-running days, molasses has been consumed in New England. We use it in almost everything, like this great barbecued chicken.

¼ cup dark molasses
¼ cup tomato puree
2 tablespoons olive oil
1 tablespoon cider vinegar
1 teaspoon onion powder
½ teaspoon peeled and
    finely chopped garlic
1 teaspoon salt
1 teaspoon Dijon mustard
¾ teaspoon chile paste
4 boneless chicken breast
    halves, with or without
    skin, pounded slightly

1. In a large bowl, whisk together the molasses, tomato puree, olive oil, cider vinegar, onion powder, garlic, salt, mustard, and chile paste.

2. Add the chicken breasts and gently toss together. Cover the bowl and refrigerate for 3 hours.

3. Preheat a grill to medium. Place the chicken breasts on the grill and cook for 3 minutes. Using tongs or a fork, rotate the breasts 90 degrees to form grill marks. Cook for another 4 minutes then flip the breasts over. Lower the heat to medium-low. After 3 minutes, rotate the breasts 90 degrees to form another set of grill marks. Cook for another 3 minutes or until the juices run clear when you insert a knife into the thickest part of the breast. Keep the grill covered at all times except when rotating or flipping the chicken.

4. Remove the chicken breasts from the grill and serve.

5. Don't have a grill? Sear the breast halves golden brown in a little bit of olive oil in a nonstick sauté pan, approximately 3–4 minutes per side, then roast in a preheated 375°F oven for about 20 minutes.

Serves 4

Melted Cheddar and Mushroom Topped Chicken Piccata with Madeira Sauce

This dish is great if you're in a hurry because the chicken cooks so quickly. The Madeira provides a touch of sweetness that complements the mushrooms and cheese.

1. On a clean work surface, divide the breasts in half and then slice each half from end to end lengthwise, to form four cutlets. Place a sheet of plastic wrap or waxed paper over the cutlets and gently pound with a meat hammer or the side of a cleaver. Set aside.

2. In a large, shallow bowl, combine the flour, salt, and pepper.

3. Heat a 10-inch sauté pan over medium-high heat. Add the butter.

4. Dredge the chicken cutlets in the flour mixture, shaking off any excess. When the butter starts to brown, place the cutlets in the pan and sauté until golden brown, about 3 minutes.

5. Flip the cutlets over, then add the shallot and mushrooms. Cook for another 3 minutes.

6. Add the Madeira, lower the heat, and simmer for 5 minutes.

7. Arrange the cheese over the top of each cutlet, cover the pan, and cook until the cheese melts, about 1 minute.

8. Divide the cutlets onto four plates, top with the mushroom sauce, and serve.

Serves 4

2 boneless, skinless chicken breasts halves, about ½ pound each
¾ cup all-purpose flour
½ teaspoon salt
½ teaspoon white pepper
4 tablespoons (½ stick) butter
1 shallot, peeled and chopped
1 cup button mushrooms, sliced
1 cup Madeira
4 slices cheddar

The Candlelight's Chicken Potpie with Flaky Crust

The first restaurant I ever worked at as a cook served chicken potpie. People loved it. I had never before seen potpie with the crust cooked separately.

1 sheet frozen puff pastry, thawed and refrigerated

1½ cups chicken broth

1 small white onion, peeled and diced

1 celery stalk, trimmed and diced

1 carrot, peeled and diced

2 medium-sized Yukon Gold potatoes, peeled and cubed

2 boneless, skinless chicken breast halves, cut into ½-inch cubes

2 tablespoons cornstarch

¼ cup water

½ cup sweet peas

1½ teaspoons chopped fresh thyme

1½ teaspoons chopped fresh parsley

¼ cup light cream

¾ teaspoon salt

½ teaspoon white pepper

1. Preheat the oven to 375°F.

2. Cut the puff pastry into four equal squares. Arrange the pastry squares on a lightly floured cookie sheet and prick them with a fork. Bake for 35 minutes or until golden brown. Set aside, keeping warm.

3. Place the chicken broth, onion, celery, carrot, and potatoes in a large saucepot. Bring to a gentle boil over medium heat, and simmer for 10 minutes. Add the cubed chicken and cook for an additional 10 minutes.

4. In a small bowl, mix the cornstarch and water. Slowly stir the mixture into the pot, stirring constantly for 1 minute.

5. Stir in the peas, thyme, parsley, and light cream. Season with the salt and pepper.

6. Remove from the heat, divide the mixture into four bowls, and top with the puff pastry. Serve immediately.

Serves 4

Pan-Fried Chicken Livers and Onions

My mom's two favorite ingredients are chicken livers and onions. This dish is my variation on *fegato alla Veneziana,* a popular liver-and-onion dish in Venice, Italy, where I worked for a summer.

2 tablespoons butter, divided

2 tablespoons olive oil, divided

1 large onion, peeled and thinly sliced

1 clove garlic, peeled and crushed

½ cup sifted all-purpose flour

1 teaspoon salt

½ teaspoon ground black pepper

½ teaspoon ground cardamom

1 pound chicken livers, cut into lobes

¾ cup Marsala

¼ cup washed and chopped parsley

1. In a medium-sized sauté pan, over medium-high heat, melt 1 tablespoon of the butter and 1 tablespoon of the olive oil.

2. When the butter bubbles, add the onion and garlic; sauté until golden brown, about 4–5 minutes. Remove from the pan and reserve.

3. In a medium-sized bowl, combine the flour, salt, pepper, and cardamom. Dredge the livers in the flour mix, shaking them gently to remove any excess.

4. Return the pan to the stove on medium heat. Add the remaining tablespoons of butter and oil. When the butter starts to bubble, add the livers.

5. Cook the livers until golden brown, about 4 minutes, then turn them over and repeat the process.

6. Remove the livers from the pan. Add the Marsala and reduce the wine by half, scraping up any bits that have formed on the bottom of the pan with a wooden spoon.

7. When the wine has reduced, return the onions and livers to the pan, gently reheat for a minute, sprinkle with the parsley, and serve.

Serves 4

Roasted Turkey, Sage, and Canadian Brown Bread Meatballs

Eat these meatballs by themselves, on a salad, in a crusty roll, or with your favorite pasta and tomato sauce. I grew up making this with anadama bread, a cornmeal molasses bread popular in New England, but Canadian brown bread works just as well and is easier to find.

1. Preheat the oven to 375°F.

2. In a medium-sized sauté pan, melt the butter over medium heat. When it starts to bubble, add the onion and sage. Cook, stirring occasionally, until the onion turns light brown, about 5–6 minutes. Set aside and cool.

3. In a large mixing bowl, beat together the egg and cream. Add the bread; stir to combine until the bread softens.

4. Add the ground turkey and the onion-and-sage mixture. Season with salt and pepper.

5. Line a cookie sheet with waxed paper. Brush with the olive oil.

6. Roll the mixture into 2-inch balls (you should get about twelve) and arrange on the cookie sheet. Bake for 20 minutes. Remove from the oven and serve.

Serves 4

1 tablespoon butter
1 onion, peeled and diced
1 teaspoon chopped fresh sage
1 egg
¼ cup light cream
3 slices Canadian brown bread (or other brown bread), crusts removed, cut into small pieces
1 pound ground turkey (a mix of dark and white meats if possible; otherwise dark)
1 teaspoon salt
½ teaspoon white pepper
2 tablespoons olive oil

DANIEL'S TIP:
When you're making meatballs or meat loaf, sauté a tiny bit of the meat mixture beforehand in a small pan to see whether or not you need to correct the seasonings.

Brown Sugar and Lime Roasted Duck Breast

I like combining sour and sweet in marinades and rubs. Tart lime and rich brown sugar make a delicious and easy-to-prepare glazed duck breast.

3 tablespoons brown sugar
Juice and zest of 2 limes
½ teaspoon ground black pepper
1 teaspoon salt
4 Long Island duck breast halves

1. Preheat the oven to 400°F.

2. In a bowl, combine the brown sugar, lime juice, lime zest, pepper, and salt.

3. With a sharp knife, score the fat side of the duck breast halves to form tight cross marks. Be careful not to cut into the meat.

4. Heat a large sauté pan over medium heat. When the pan is hot, lay the duck breast halves, fat-side down, in the pan and cook for 7 minutes. After a few minutes, carefully drain the fat into a heatproof container.

5. Toss the duck breasts with the brown sugar and lime mixture. Arrange them, fat-side up, on a wire rack in a roasting pan. Pour 1 cup water into the bottom of the roasting pan—the water should not touch the bottom of the rack.

6. Roast the duck breasts 20 minutes for medium-rare. Let them rest for 5 minutes before serving.

Serves 4

DANIEL'S TIP:
Leftover duck fat makes an excellent substitute for bacon fat for frying potatoes, vegetables, or the ingredients for stuffing.

MEATS

Since colonial days, meat has been a staple of the New England diet. Even today we love our grilled steaks and slow-braised stews. When I was growing up, my dad used to bring home a lot of wild game. We never thought of it as living off the land; it was just living.

Cumin Rubbed Roasted Pork Tenderloin with Pear Ginger Compote

Pork tenderloin is the easiest pork to cook. It's flavorful, fast, and not very fatty. It makes a wonderful foil for fruit, like this ginger pear compote.

Pear Compote

3 medium-sized pears (any fresh pear will do), peeled, cored, and small diced

1 tablespoon sugar

1 teaspoon peeled and finely chopped fresh ginger

½ cup water

Place the chopped pears, sugar, ginger, and water in a small saucepan. Bring to a boil, then lower the heat, partially cover the pan, and simmer for 30 minutes or until the pears are tender. Remove from the stove and keep warm.

Pork Tenderloin

2 (1-pound) boneless pork tenderloins

1 teaspoon olive oil

1 teaspoon powdered cumin

1 teaspoon powdered coriander

½ teaspoon powdered cardamom

1 teaspoon sugar

1 teaspoon salt

1 teaspoon cracked black pepper

1. Preheat the oven to 375°F.

2. Rub both tenderloins with the olive oil.

3. In a shallow bowl, mix together the cumin, coriander, cardamom, sugar, salt, and black pepper. Dredge the tenderloins in the spice rub so that they are entirely coated.

4. Place the tenderloins on a rack in a roasting pan. Roast the pork loins for 20 minutes for medium. Rest 5 minutes before slicing. Serve, topped with the pear compote.

Serves 4

Pork Chops with Corn Bread Dressing

The difference between dressings and stuffings is that dressings are served on the side while stuffings are cooked inside the main course. In this recipe, I sear the pork chops first, before roasting them, and make a savory jus from their drippings to liven up the corn bread dressing.

Pork Chops

4 (7-ounce) bone-in pork
  chops
1 teaspoon salt
1 teaspoon cracked black
  pepper
1 tablespoon butter
¼ cup water

1. Preheat the oven to 375°F.

2. Season the pork chops with the salt and pepper.

3. Heat a large cast iron or heavy-bottomed sauté pan over high heat until very hot. Add the tablespoon of butter. As soon as the butter bubbles, add the pork chops, in batches if necessary, and sauté until golden on both sides, approximately 3 minutes a side. Add another tablespoon of butter to the pan if you're sautéing a second batch.

4. Transfer the chops to a greased or waxed paper–lined roasting pan.

5. Add the water to the sauté pan and bring to a boil while stirring. Remove from the heat, strain, and reserve the liquid (jus).

Corn Bread Dressing

1 teaspoon butter
2 cups crumbled corn bread
  (see page 8)
2 tablespoons Thai sweet
  chile sauce
2 eggs, beaten
½ cup milk
1 teaspoon salt
Pork jus

1. Grease a small ovenproof casserole with the butter.

2. In a large bowl, combine the crumbled corn bread, chile sauce, eggs, milk, salt, and the pork jus. Pour into the greased casserole.

3. Place the seared pork chops and dressing in the oven. After 12 minutes, remove the chops. Cook the dressing for an additional 5 minutes while the pork rests.

4. Serve immediately, pouring any accumulated pork juices from the roasting pan on top of the dressing.

Serves 4

Dry-Rubbed Pork Ribs

This dry rub can be used on everything from chicken to grilled steaks. The recipe can easily be multiplied or divided. These ribs are a tradition at my backyard barbecues.

In a shallow bowl, combine the salt, pepper, sugar, cumin, onion powder, garlic powder, ground fennel, paprika, and ground coriander. Set aside.

1. Preheat the oven to 350°F.

2. Remove and discard the membrane from the underside of the ribs with a sharp knife.

3. In a large kettle, bring the water, salt, black pepper, coriander, and ribs to a gentle boil. Lower the heat and simmer for 40 minutes.

4. Remove the ribs from kettle and, when they're cool enough to handle, rub them top and bottom with the olive oil. Sprinkle half of the rub on the bottom of the ribs, then the remaining rub on the top.

5. Place the ribs on a rack in a roasting pan and bake for 45 minutes.

Serves 6

Rub

1 tablespoon coarse salt
2 tablespoons cracked black pepper
2 tablespoons sugar
2 teaspoons ground cumin
2 teaspoons onion powder
2 teaspoons garlic powder
2 teaspoons ground fennel
2 teaspoons paprika
2 teaspoons ground coriander

Ribs

2 pork rib racks, about 2 pounds each
4 quarts (16 cups) water
2 tablespoons salt
2 tablespoons black pepper
2 tablespoons coriander seeds
2 tablespoons olive oil

Wine and Food

My love of cooking is only equaled by my love of wine. For the past twenty-five years, I've been able to combine the two passions in the Boston Wine Festival, a three-month-long series of winemaker dinners that is the oldest event of its kind in the country, and at the Boston Harbor Hotel's Meritage restaurant, with its unique wine-inspired menu.

While most people go out to dinner and select wine to complement the food they've ordered, at the Wine Festival and at Meritage, we reverse the formula; the food is designed to complement the wines. If you think about it, switching the emphasis from food to wine makes perfect sense—and once you've eaten this way, your palate will agree.

When I'm creating menus to accompany specific wines, I begin by grouping the wines according to their most basic characteristics: sparkling wines, light whites, full-bodied whites, fruity reds, spicy/earthy reds, and robust reds. I taste each wine, looking for flavors in the glass that remind me of specific culinary ingredients: vanilla, fennel, smoke, citrus, rosemary, or black pepper, for example. Then I come up with dishes that balance and enhance those ingredients and flavors. Believe me, when you're eating something meant to go with the exact wine you're drinking, both the dish and the wine taste better.

Try it yourself with some of the recipes in this book. Make the crab cakes and open up a bottle of Prosecco or Champagne. Serve the creamy onion soup with a glass of oaky Chardonnay. Accompany the maple and mustard glazed lamb sirloin with a Bordeaux or the grilled prime filet with a California Cabernet. When wine and food are properly paired, it's like the best marriages—the combination of the two is stronger than the individual components.

My friend Howie Rubin describes the proper pairing of wine and food as "Climbing the Stairway to Heaven." Drink a chilled French Sancerre alongside a half dozen freshly shucked Wellfleet oysters on the half shell and tell me if you don't think he's right.

"Melt in Your Mouth" Meat Loaf

The secret to making good meat loaf is a panade of bread, milk, and egg, which ensures that the meat remains moist and tender when it's baking.

1. Preheat the oven to 400°F.

2. In a small sauté pan over medium heat, melt the butter. Add the onion and garlic and slowly cook until tender, about 4–5 minutes, being careful not to let the onion turn color. Remove from the heat and cool.

3. In a medium-sized bowl, beat together the egg and milk. Add the bread and soak for 5 minutes. Add the Worcestershire sauce, Tabasco sauce, tomato puree, and cooled onion and garlic; stir together. Then add the ground beef and salt and thoroughly combine.

4. Gently form the meat mixture into a log, approximately 3 inches in diameter. Lightly oil a 14-inch sheet of parchment or waxed paper. Roll the paper tightly over the meatloaf, oiled-side in.

5. Place the paper-covered loaf on a cookie sheet and bake for 25 minutes. Remove from the oven and rest for 5 minutes. Remove and discard the parchment paper. Slice and serve.

1½ tablespoons butter
1 small onion, peeled and minced
1 clove garlic, peeled and minced
1 egg
½ cup milk
4 slices white bread, crusts removed, cut into pieces
1 teaspoon Worcestershire sauce
½ teaspoon Tabasco sauce
2 tablespoons tomato puree
1 pound 85% lean ground beef
1¼ teaspoons salt

Serves 4

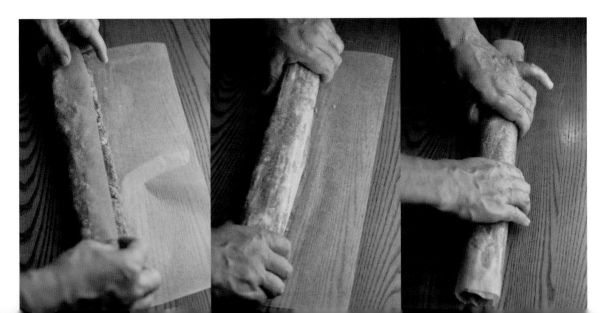

Maple and Mustard Glazed Lamb Sirloin

Lamb sirloin is the lamb loin with a cap of fat on one side. Ask your butcher. If you can't find sirloin, you can substitute lamb chops—figure one meaty chop per person.

6 tablespoons maple syrup

6 tablespoons Dijon
   mustard

2 (1-pound) lamb sirloins (or
   4 meaty lamb chops)

¾ teaspoon salt

1 teaspoon black pepper

2 teaspoons olive oil

1. Preheat the oven to 425°F.

2. In a large bowl, mix together the maple syrup and Dijon mustard. Set aside.

3. Season the lamb with the salt and pepper.

4. Heat a large sauté pan over high heat. Add the olive oil and, when the oil starts to smoke, add the lamb, fat-side down. Sear the lamb until golden brown on both sides, about 3 minutes per side.

5. Remove the lamb from the hot pan. Carefully roll the sirloins (or chops) in the glaze, making sure both sides are covered. Place the lamb on a rack in a roasting pan. Pour about 1 cup of water in the bottom of the roasting pan, making sure that the water doesn't touch the rack.

6. Roast the lamb in the oven for 10 minutes. Spoon the remaining glaze over the top of the lamb and continue roasting for another 10–12 minutes for medium-rare. Let the meat rest for 5 minutes before slicing and serving. If you're using chops, serve whole.

Serves 3

DANIEL'S TIP:
When roasting any meat or poultry using high heat, put it on a rack and pour water in the bottom of the roasting pan to prevent the grease from the meat from burning on the bottom of the pan and smoking up your kitchen. Make sure the water never touches the rack and replenish the water if necessary during cooking.

Garlic-Studded Leg of Lamb with Easy Mint Jus

I have fond memories of my grandmother's roast leg of lamb, particularly at Easter. But don't save this recipe only for special occasions; it's a snap to prepare and delicious at any family gathering.

Lamb

1 (2-pound) boneless leg of lamb, tied (ask your butcher to tie it for you)
5 cloves garlic, peeled and cut in half lengthwise
1 tablespoon olive oil
2 teaspoons salt
1 teaspoon black pepper

1. Preheat the oven to 425°F.

2. Place the lamb on a clean, dry work surface and, with the point of a sharp paring knife, make ten 1-inch-deep incisions equally spaced over the roast. Insert half a garlic clove into each incision. Rub the lamb with olive oil and sprinkle with salt and pepper.

3. Place the lamb on a rack in a roasting pan. Pour about 1 cup of water into the bottom of the pan, making sure that the water doesn't touch the rack.

4. Place the lamb in the oven and roast for 15 minutes at 425°F. Reduce the heat to 375°F and roast an additional 45 minutes for medium-rare or until a thermometer inserted into the meat reads 120°F.

5. Remove the meat from the oven and let it rest for 10 minutes before carving.

1. Pour the drippings from the lamb pan into a 1-cup measuring cup. If the drippings measure less than 1 cup, add water to equal 1 cup.

2. In a small saucepan over high heat, bring the cup of drippings, the mint, honey, vinegar, and salt to a boil. Lower the heat and simmer the mixture for 10 minutes. Serve with the sliced lamb.

Serves 6

Jus

Lamb drippings

Leaves from 4 sprigs mint, chopped

2 tablespoons honey

2 tablespoons cider vinegar

½ teaspoon salt

21 Club

At the age of twenty-seven, I was named executive chef at New York City's famed 21 Club. "21" is a New York dining and drinking institution that dates back to Prohibition. In 1985, it was purchased by financier Marshall Cogan. He gave the restaurant a much-needed face-lift and hired Alain Sailhac, who had been my boss and mentor at Le Cirque. I went along with Sailhac. After a year, he left and I was promoted to executive chef. There were guys in the kitchen who had been working on the line longer than I had been alive.

I worked as executive chef at 21 for a year. It was an honor to work in such a legendary institution. There were a lot of firsts for me there. It was my first job at the helm. I interacted with guests, making my first nervous appearances in the dining room. Most exciting, I began my food and wine-pairing odyssey with intimate wine dinners hidden away in the prohibition-era, secret wine cellar.

There were two restaurants: an upstairs fine dining room where I had complete freedom, but the downstairs bar was to remain the same, serving classics like the "21" Burger, Chicken Hash, and "Speakeasy" Steak Tartare.

In the end, I wanted more freedom than I could find in a restaurant defined by its history, so I moved next back to New England to embark on the future of a sparkling new hotel on the Boston waterfront.

Rowes Wharf Caramelized Onion and Cheese Filled Cheeseburgers

Serve these burgers "with a surprise inside" on your favorite roll or bun. Rotating the burgers every 3 minutes on the grill will give you a nice crosshatch pattern.

1 tablespoon butter

1 medium-sized onion, peeled and thinly sliced

½ cup grated cheddar cheese

1¼ pounds 85% lean ground beef

1 tablespoon olive oil

1 teaspoon salt

½ teaspoon cracked black pepper

1. Preheat a grill.

2. In a medium-sized sauté pan, melt the butter over medium heat. Add the onion and sauté, stirring often, until the onion turns golden brown, 7–8 minutes.

3. Transfer the onion to a small bowl and cool. Stir in the grated cheddar.

4. Form the ground beef into four equal-sized balls. Make a well in the center of each ball. Fill each well with an equal amount of the onion-cheddar mixture. Fold the meat over to fully enclose the onion-cheddar mixture, making sure that the meat is the same thickness on both the top and bottom. Gently pat the balls into patties.

5. Rub both sides of the patties with olive oil and season with salt and pepper.

6. Place the burgers on the hot grill. Sear for 3 minutes, then rotate 90 degrees and sear for another 3 minutes. Carefully flip the burgers over and sear for 3 minutes. Rotate the burgers 90 degrees and finish searing for a final 3 minutes for medium-rare.

Serves 4

Beef and Winter Vegetable Stew

When I was a kid, my mom would simmer stew all night on our woodstove. You add the red wine before you add the water because you want to burn off all the alcohol. You add the vegetables at the end because the meat takes at least three times longer to cook than the vegetables; if you were to throw them all in together at the beginning, your vegetables would be overcooked. And you add the kale at the very end to keep it green.

2 tablespoons olive oil

1 teaspoon salt

2 pounds cubed chuck stew meat

2 tablespoons flour

½ teaspoon ground cumin

½ teaspoon ground black pepper

½ teaspoon ground cardamom

1 clove garlic, peeled and chopped

2 cups red wine

5 cups chicken stock

2 bay leaves

2 medium-sized Yukon Gold potatoes, peeled and cubed

2 carrots, peeled and cut into ¼-inch slices

1 large onion, peeled and cubed

1 white turnip, peeled and cubed

1 cup chopped green kale

1. In a large Dutch oven or saucepan, heat the oil and salt over medium-high heat. When the mixture starts to smoke, add the meat cubes (see Daniel's Tip).

2. Let the meat sear, without stirring, until it's golden brown on one side, about 5–6 minutes. Turn the cubes over and sear the other side for another 5 or so minutes—don't rush the process.

3. When the meat is browned, sift the flour, cumin, pepper, cardamom, and garlic into the pot. Stir to incorporate. Cook for 1 minute and add the red wine. Stir well, bring to a boil, reduce the heat to medium-low, cover, and cook until the red wine is reduced by half, about 15 minutes.

4. Stir in the chicken stock and bay leaves. Keep stirring until the liquid thickens slightly. Raise the heat, bring to a boil, then lower the heat and simmer, covered, until the meat is tender, approximately 1 hour.

5. Add the potatoes, carrots, onion, and turnip; simmer, covered, for 25 minutes or until thoroughly cooked. Add the kale and simmer for an additional 5 minutes.

6. Remove the bay leaves and serve immediately.

Serves 6

DANIEL'S TIP:

Anytime you want to sear meat (or poultry, fish, or even vegetables), add the salt called for in the recipe to the oil in the pan and heat, over medium-high heat, to the smoking point. The salt will dissolve and coat the bottom of the pan to form a nonstick barrier between the pan and whatever it is you're cooking. That nonstick surface will last indefinitely until you add liquid. Once you've added liquid, if you're going to continue cooking the dish in that pan, you'll want to adjust any additional salt accordingly.

Cocoa and Coffee Rubbed Grilled Flank Steak

Chocolate has been manufactured in New England since 1765, when James Baker and John Hannon opened a waterpowered chocolate factory in the Dorchester neighborhood of Boston. This grilled flank steak is my American take on mole.

1. Preheat the oven to 400°F.

2. In a small bowl, combine the cocoa powder, coffee, honey, wine, cardamom, brown sugar, onion powder, and garlic powder. Mix together thoroughly to form a paste.

3. Season both sides of the flank steak with the salt and pepper.

4. In a large sauté pan over high heat, heat the olive oil to the smoking point. Sear the steak until it's golden brown on both sides, approximately 6 minutes a side. Remove the steak from the pan and let it rest for 5 minutes. Coat the steak on both sides with the cocoa paste.

5. Place the steak on a rack in a roasting pan. Pour about 1 cup of water into the bottom of the pan, making sure the water does not touch the rack.

6. Roast the flank steak for 12–13 minutes for medium-rare.

7. Remove the steak from the oven. Let it rest for 6 minutes before carving. Slice the steak at a 45-degree angle, cutting against the grain.

Serves 4

2 tablespoons cocoa powder
2 tablespoons instant coffee
½ teaspoon honey
2 tablespoons red wine
½ teaspoon ground cardamom
1 tablespoon dark brown sugar
1 teaspoon onion powder
1 teaspoon garlic powder
1 (1¾-pound) flank steak
1 teaspoon salt
½ teaspoon black pepper
2 tablespoons olive oil

DANIEL'S TIP:
Whatever the cut, whatever the meat, slicing against the grain yields more tender meat.

Grilled Prime Filet with Horseradish Sauce and Red Wine Syrup

This has been one of my signature dishes in Meritage since it opened in 2002. The sweet red wine syrup contrasts with the spicy horseradish sauce in a striking, streaked red and white presentation.

Horseradish Sauce

1 teaspoon butter
1 small shallot, peeled and sliced
1 cup light cream
1 tablespoon water
½ teaspoon cornstarch
1 tablespoon pickled white horseradish
¾ teaspoon salt

1. In a small saucepan, melt the butter over low heat. When the butter bubbles, add the shallot and gently cook until translucent, about 4 minutes, stirring occasionally.

2. Add the light cream, increase the heat to medium, and bring to a boil. As soon as it comes to a boil, lower the heat.

3. Meanwhile, in a small bowl, stir together the water and cornstarch. Whisk this mixture into the cream, and simmer for 1 minute, whisking constantly.

4. Stir in the horseradish and season with salt. Set aside, keeping warm.

Red Wine Syrup

2 cups full-bodied red wine (like Cabernet)
2 tablespoons honey

1. In a stainless-steel pot, over high heat, bring the wine to a boil. Lower the heat to a simmer and reduce until about ¼ cup of syrupy liquid remains, approximately 30 minutes.

2. Stir in the honey and set aside.

Filets

4 (7-ounce) prime filets mignons
3 tablespoons olive oil, divided
Salt
Cracked black pepper

1. Preheat the oven to 400°F.

2. Rub the filets with 1 tablespoon of the olive oil and season with the salt and cracked black pepper.

3. In a large sauté pan over high heat, heat the remaining 2 tablespoons olive oil. Add the filets and sear until dark brown on both sides, about 3 minutes per side.

4. Arrange the filets on a rack in a roasting pan. Pour about 1 cup water into the bottom of the pan, making sure that the water doesn't touch the rack.

5. Roast the steaks for 14 minutes for medium-rare.

6. Rest the steaks for 5 minutes, then arrange on four plates. Pour horseradish sauce over the steaks, followed by a drizzling of red wine syrup.

Serves 4

Red Wine and Chinese Five Spice—Braised Boneless Beef Short Ribs

This is one of those rib-sticking-good winter suppers that beg for mashed potatoes made with lots of butter and cream or soft polenta.

6 (6-ounce) boneless beef short ribs
2 tablespoons Chinese five-spice powder or ground fennel seeds
1 teaspoon salt
½ teaspoon black pepper
1 tablespoon olive oil
1 small onion, peeled and chopped
1 carrot, peeled and chopped
1 celery rib, ends trimmed and chopped
2 cups red wine
4 garlic cloves, peeled and chopped
2 cups chicken stock
2 cups crushed tomatoes, fresh or canned

1. Trim and discard the excess fat from the short ribs. Season the short ribs with the Chinese five-spice powder or ground fennel seeds, salt, and pepper.

2. Heat the oil over medium-high heat in a large Dutch oven or pot. Sear the short ribs, fatty-side down, in the oil until golden brown, approximately 5 minutes per side.

3. Add the chopped onion, carrot, and celery; cook for 4 minutes, stirring frequently to prevent the vegetables from burning.

4. Add the red wine and garlic, loosening any bits sticking to the bottom of the pan with a wooden spoon. Cover and cook until the wine is reduced by half, approximately 20 minutes.

5. Add the chicken stock and crushed tomatoes. Bring to a boil, reduce the heat, cover, and simmer for approximately 2½ hours or until the short ribs are fork-tender, stirring occasionally and carefully skimming off any excess fat with a spoon when necessary.

Serves 6

VEGETABLES

You know what time of year it is in New England by the vegetables on your plate. I look forward to the rites of spring, the fiddleheads and asparagus, moving on to summer's bounty of corn and tomatoes and the autumn harvest of squashes and root vegetables that we'll store and cook with throughout winter. And, of course, the mushrooms I forage, from spring to late fall.

Wild Mushroom Polenta

If you don't have access to wild mushrooms, this polenta is terrific with the mushrooms you can find in your local supermarket: cremini, portobellos, shiitake, even button. Don't be put off by the three-part recipe. If you make the sauce first, then the polenta, and finally the mushrooms, the dish will be on the table in under 30 minutes.

Sauce

4 cups chicken stock
½ cup heavy cream
¼ teaspoon salt
¼ teaspoon white pepper

1. In a heavy-bottomed saucepan over medium-high heat, reduce the chicken stock to 1 cup.

2. Whisk in the heavy cream and simmer until the sauce thickens slightly. Season with salt and pepper. Remove from the heat and keep warm.

Polenta

2 cups milk
4 tablespoons (½ stick) butter
½ cup white cornmeal
1 tablespoon chopped fresh herbs (preferably thyme, rosemary, and/or parsley)
½ teaspoon salt
¼ teaspoon white pepper

1. In a large saucepan over medium-high heat, bring the milk and butter to a gentle boil.

2. Slowly pour in the cornmeal, whisking constantly to avoid lumps. Continue to whisk until the polenta starts to thicken. Simmer for 15 minutes over low heat, stirring occasionally. The polenta should be the consistency of thick porridge.

3. Remove from the heat; stir in the chopped herbs and salt and pepper to taste. Keep warm, covered.

DANIEL'S TIP:
Most mushrooms are between 80 and 90 percent water, so you don't want to wash them. Instead, gently brush off any dirt that may be clinging to them. Then slice the mushrooms and sauté over very high heat. You want to remove the water content as quickly as possible to allow for caramelization and color—which add flavor. Also, don't crowd the pan; the mushroom water will pool up on the bottom of the pan, preventing caramelization and color.

1. Heat a large, heavy-bottomed sauté pan over high heat.

2. When the pan is very hot, add the butter and quickly follow with the mushrooms, garlic, and shallot. Sauté, tossing occasionally to avoid burning, until the mushrooms are lightly browned, about 6–7 minutes. Season with salt and pepper.

3. Serve over the polenta with a generous ladle of sauce.

Serves 2 as an entree, 4 as a side dish

Mushrooms

2 tablespoons cold butter, cut into small chunks

1 pound assorted wild mushrooms, cleaned and thinly sliced

1 teaspoon finely chopped garlic

1 shallot, peeled and thinly sliced

½ teaspoon salt

¼ teaspoon white pepper

Mushrooming

Growing up in the northwest woods of Maine, I always foraged for wild edibles—fiddleheads, ramps, wild strawberries, wild asparagus, pussy willows—but never for mushrooms. There was always the possibility they could be poisonous.

I first started foraging for mushrooms when I was a teenager and realized that the wild mushrooms being delivered to the restaurant where I was working in Skowhegan were the same ones I would see when I was exploring the surrounding woods. I bought a couple of mushrooming books. That was the beginning. But the reading and education never ended.

Today I go out looking for mushrooms from the end of April to the beginning of December. Where? Well, you're only allowed to reveal where you go mushrooming on your deathbed. And then only to your eldest child. And then only if he or she has led an exemplary life. And then only if you're absolutely sure you're going to die. Okay, I do make exceptions when I want the company.

I've identified well over five hundred places across New England where edible mushrooms grow wild, that I visit year after year. I bring home stropharia (which are called wine-caps), morel mushrooms (both blond and dark), chicken mushrooms, lobster mushrooms, hen-of-the-woods, seven or eight different types of boletes, black trumpets, chanterelles and yellow footed chanterelles, and hedgehogs.

I leave the house between 2:00 and 3:00 a.m. so that I'm in the woods just as the sun goes up. My wife, Julianna, always asks me, "Can they only be picked at dawn?" But this way I can get in a full day of foraging before I go off to work. And also it's cooler in the morning, which is better for foraging.

A good day of mushrooming is 50 pounds or more. A great day is 200 pounds or more. And my best day ever was 440 pounds. I could have had more but my then pastry chef George, who was with me, accidentally slammed his thumb in the hatchback of my Toyota Camry on a deserted dirt road trying to escape a vicious dog that appeared out of nowhere. I kept going for a few more hours but George was in no shape to continue. He ended up getting two pins implanted vertically in his thumb and was out of work for several weeks.

George's wife—who is a nurse—read me the riot act. But it was a memorable day of mushrooming.

Maine Potato and Chive Cakes

These cakes are easy to make, moist, and delicious. Not only are they a great alternative to mashed potatoes, but you can cut them into circles, squares, or any shape you want to liven up your plates during a dinner party. You can make them the night before, throw them in the fridge before you go to bed, and cook them up in the morning—they're fabulous with eggs.

3–4 Yukon Gold potatoes, peeled (about 1¼ pounds)
3 tablespoons heavy cream
2 egg yolks
¼ cup chopped chives
3 tablespoons butter, divided
¾ teaspoon salt
¼ teaspoon white pepper

1. Cut the potatoes into ¼-inch slices. Cook in boiling water until tender. Drain the potatoes until very dry, and mash until smooth. Let rest for 5 minutes. Stir in the cream, egg yolks, chives, and 2 tablespoons of the butter. Season with salt and pepper.

2. Pour the potatoes into an 8-inch round cake pan lined with plastic wrap. Cover with plastic wrap and pat down with your hands to form a smooth surface. Refrigerate for at least 4 hours.

3. Preheat the oven to 350°F.

4. Cut the cold potato cake into four portions. Heat the remaining tablespoon of butter in a large, nonstick, ovenproof sauté pan over medium-high heat. When the butter starts to bubble, add the cakes and sauté until they're golden on both sides, about 3–4 minutes per side.

5. Place the sauté pan in the oven for 5 minutes. Remove and serve immediately.

Serves 4

Summertime Sweet Corn Pudding

When you're making this pudding, ask your farmer at your local farmers' market for the sweetest corn he or she has. Frozen or canned corn will not work with this dish. And by the way, if you don't have ramekins, you can make this in a buttered 2-quart casserole as well.

1. Preheat the oven to 375°F.

2. Shuck the corn and remove the kernels (see page 58).

3. Butter eight 4-ounce ramekins. Divide the corn kernels among the ramekins.

4. In a bowl, whisk together the heavy cream and eggs. Season with salt and pepper. Pour the mixture over the corn.

5. Place the ramekins in a roasting pan just large enough to hold them. Bake for 25–30 minutes or until the tops are golden brown and a knife inserted in the middle of the pudding comes out clean.

Serves 8

4 ears fresh sweet corn
2 cups heavy cream
3 eggs
¾ teaspoon salt
½ teaspoon white pepper

Creamy Red Bliss Potatoes

If you're looking for a change from mashed, you've come to the right place. This dish is easily doubled or tripled for Thanksgiving.

1½ pounds red bliss, Maine, or other new potatoes, cut into quarters
½ tablespoon cornstarch
1½ tablespoons water
1 cup light cream
1 teaspoon salt
½ teaspoon black pepper

1. Fill a large saucepan with water and bring to a boil. Add the potatoes, lower the heat to a simmer, and cook the potatoes until tender, approximately 15 minutes. Drain the potatoes and set aside.

2. In a small bowl, dissolve the cornstarch in the water.

3. In a second saucepan over medium-high heat, bring the cream to a boil. Lower the heat to a simmer, whisk in the cornstarch mixture, and cook for 1 minute, stirring constantly.

4. Add the potatoes to the saucepan. Toss with the cream and season with the salt and pepper. Serve immediately.

Serves 5

Roasted Winter Root Vegetables

This is another cold-weather dish that couldn't be simpler to prepare. Plus, it tastes good and it's good for you. The heat of the roasted vegetables wilts the kale just enough so that it retains a bit of crunch.

2 medium peeled carrots
1 small peeled butternut
   squash
1 small peeled rutabaga
1 medium peeled red onion
1 cup chopped washed kale
¼ cup olive oil
¾ teaspoon salt
¼ teaspoon black pepper

1. Preheat the oven to 425°F.

2. Cut the carrots, squash, rutabaga, and onion into ½-inch pieces. You want them all to be approximately the same size. Toss the vegetables in a large bowl with the olive oil. Season with salt and pepper.

3. Spread the vegetables on a nonstick cookie sheet and bake for approximately 30 minutes or until tender. Halfway through the cooking, toss the vegetables with a spatula.

4. Return the vegetables to the bowl. Stir in the chopped kale. Cover the bowl with plastic wrap and let sit for 5 minutes. Serve.

Serves 6

Spinach and Mushroom Strada

This is a quick, Italian-inspired option when you're in the mood for quiche. It's great by itself, and especially tasty as the centerpiece of a weekend brunch.

1. Preheat the oven to 375°F.

2. In a bowl, beat together the milk, cream, and eggs. Add the bread and soak for 10 minutes.

3. In a medium-sized sauté pan over medium heat, melt the butter. When it bubbles, add the onion and sauté until light brown, approximately 5–6 minutes. Add the spinach and cook until wilted, about 2 minutes. Remove from the pan and cool.

4. Add the onion, spinach, mushrooms, salt, and pepper to the cream-and-egg mixture. Fold in the cheddar cheese. Pour the mixture into a lightly buttered 10-inch casserole dish.

5. Bake for 45–55 minutes or until golden brown and the custard has set. Rest for 10 minutes before serving.

Serves 8

1½ cups milk

½ cup light cream

5 eggs

3 slices white bread, crusts removed, diced

2 tablespoons butter

1 small white onion, peeled and diced

1 (10-ounce) bag spinach, washed, stemmed, and roughly chopped

1 cup portobello (or your favorite) mushrooms, cleaned and thinly sliced

1½ teaspoons salt

½ teaspoon white pepper

½ cup grated cheddar cheese

Crispy Mushroom and Rice Cakes

Basmati rice is lighter than the white rice used in most American kitchens and creates a tender, fluffy base for these tasty cakes. Sautéing them golden brown creates a crisp texture on the outside, and you can't go wrong with mushrooms.

1½ cups water
1 cup basmati rice
1 tablespoon butter
1½ cups cleaned and chopped assorted mushrooms
¼ cup sour cream
1 egg
1 scallion, chopped, roots discarded
½ teaspoon white pepper
1 teaspoon salt
1½ tablespoons olive oil

1. In a medium-sized pot over high heat, bring the water to a boil. Stir in the basmati rice, lower the heat to a slow simmer, and cook, covered, for approximately 12 minutes or until the water is absorbed and the rice is cooked. Remove from the heat and cool.

2. Heat a sauté pan over medium-high heat and melt the butter. When it starts to bubble, add the mushrooms. Sauté for 5 minutes or until golden brown, stirring only to prevent burning. Remove and cool.

3. In a large bowl, mix together the rice, mushrooms, sour cream, egg, scallion, and white pepper. Season with salt. Form the mixture into four equal-sized balls. Lightly pat with wet hands or a piece of plastic wrap to form cakes. Place the cakes on a dish, cover with plastic wrap, and refrigerate for 1 hour.

4. Heat the olive oil in a large, nonstick sauté pan over medium-high heat. When the oil is hot, add the rice cakes and sauté until golden brown, approximately 4 minutes per side.

Serves 4

Flash-Roasted Brussels Sprouts

This is a recipe I use with other vegetables (like butternut squash, pearl onions, parsnips, turnips, and eggplant) when I'm cooking at home with my family. Flash roasting intensifies the flavors—and the best part is that there's little to no cleanup required.

1 pound brussels sprouts
3 tablespoons olive oil
1 clove garlic, peeled and
  crushed
½ teaspoon salt
½ teaspoon black pepper

1. Place an empty cookie sheet in the oven. Preheat the oven to 425°F.

2. Remove the brown portion from the bottoms of the brussels sprouts. If sprouts are large, cut each in half; if small, leave whole.

3. In a large bowl, toss the brussels sprouts with the olive oil, garlic, salt, and pepper.

4. Carefully spread the brussels sprouts evenly over the hot cookie sheet.

5. Roast the sprouts for 7 minutes, then toss slightly with a spatula. Roast for another 10 minutes or until the sprouts are easily pierced with a sharp knife or toothpick. Serve immediately.

Serves 4

Pan-Glazed Carrots

Almost everyone growing up in New England has had glazed carrots. But my version is special because the orange juice adds a little zip.

1. In a medium-sized sauté pan over medium heat, melt the butter. When it begins to bubble, add the carrots. Cook for 5–6 minutes, stirring occasionally, until the carrots are slightly colored.

2. Add the honey, orange juice, salt, and white pepper. Cover the pan, reduce the heat to low, and cook for 8 minutes.

3. Remove the cover of the pan and turn the heat back up to medium-high. Cook, stirring often, until the pan juices reduce and thicken into a glaze, approximately 5 minutes.

2 tablespoons butter
1 pound carrots, peeled and
    cut into ¼-inch-thick slices
2 tablespoons honey
¼ cup orange juice,
    preferably fresh-squeezed
½ teaspoon salt
½ teaspoon white pepper

Serves 4

Maple Syrup and Smoky Bacon Baked Beans

My Nana S (my mother's mom) was always in her kitchen and, more often than not, there were baked beans ready to eat when I visited. My grandmother always gave me one of the onions—I like to think it's because I am her favorite.

1. In a large bowl, cover the beans with 3 cups of the water and let sit overnight, covered.

2. Preheat the oven to 325°F.

3. Place the beans and any remaining soaking water in a bean pot or ovenproof casserole with the remaining 3 cups water, molasses, maple syrup, mustard, tomato puree, bacon, onions, salt, and pepper.

4. Cover the pot or casserole and bake the beans for 3 hours, stirring occasionally and adding a small amount of additional water if necessary. You can also cook them in a crockpot—on low setting—for 8 hours.

Serves 8

1 pound northern white beans or other dry white beans
6 cups water, divided
½ cup molasses
½ cup maple syrup
¼ cup Dijon mustard
½ cup tomato puree
½ pound smoked slab bacon, cut into 8 large squares
3 small onions, peeled and cut in half
1½ teaspoons salt
1 teaspoon ground black pepper

Bread-Stuffed Baked Acorn Squash

Squash and harvesttime are synonymous in New England. This dish is great on those cold nights when you want a hearty vegetable side. It can also be served as a main course—it's that good.

1 acorn squash

3 tablespoons butter, divided

1 small onion, peeled and diced

1 garlic clove, peeled and diced

4 slices whole wheat bread, crust removed, diced

1 egg

1 sprig rosemary, chopped

⅓ cup milk

½ teaspoon black pepper

1 teaspoon salt, divided

1. Preheat the oven to 400°F.

2. Wash the squash and cut it in half, lengthwise. Remove and discard the seeds from the cavity. Cut a thin slice from the bottom of each half so they can rest firmly on a flat surface.

3. In a medium-sized sauté pan, heat 2 tablespoons of the butter over medium heat. When it begins to bubble, add the onion and garlic and sauté until lightly browned, about 4 minutes. Remove from the pan and cool.

4. In a medium-sized bowl, mix together the bread, egg, rosemary, and milk until thoroughly combined. Stir in the onions, garlic, black pepper, and ¾ teaspoon of the salt.

5. Melt the remaining tablespoon of butter and rub it over the cut sides and cavity of the squash. Sprinkle the squash with the remaining ¼ teaspoon salt. Fill the squash halves with the bread mixture.

6. Place the squash halves in a roasting pan just large enough to hold them. Fill the roasting pan with ½ inch of water.

7. Roast the squash for 70 minutes or until it's easily pierced with a fork. Add additional water if necessary.

Serves 4 as a side dish, 2 as an entree

DESSERTS

Desserts for me are all about the flavors, aromas, and seasonal fruits I remember from growing up with grandmothers who loved to bake. Pandowdies, cobblers, crisps, buckles, slumps, betties, and shortcakes may be traditional to New England, but they certainly deserve a spotlight on the national stage.

My Tapioca Pudding

Believe it or not, I probably wouldn't be the chef I am today if it hadn't been for tapioca pudding (see the sidebar). I still get as much enjoyment eating tapioca today as I did when I used to make it as an eleven-year-old, visiting my grandparents. Folding in the meringue lightens up the pudding.

2¾ cups whole milk

3 tablespoons Minute Tapioca

1½ teaspoons vanilla extract

¼ teaspoon allspice

2 eggs

5 tablespoons sugar, divided

1. In a small saucepot over medium-high heat, bring the milk, tapioca, vanilla, and allspice to a gentle boil, stirring occasionally to prevent clumping.

2. Separate the eggs. In small bowl, beat together the yolks and 2 tablespoons of the sugar. Vigorously whisking, slowly pour half of the hot milk into the yolk mixture, being careful not to let the yolks overcook.

3. Whisking constantly, pour the yolk-and-milk mixture back into the pot; cook, over low heat, stirring constantly until the mixture thickens to the consistency of heavy cream. Do not let it boil. When the mixture has thickened, remove the pot from the heat, cover, and cool to room temperature.

4. Meanwhile, in a clean bowl, using an electric mixer or whisk, beat together the egg whites and the remaining 3 tablespoons of sugar to form soft peaks.

5. Fold the whites into the pudding and divide among six serving bowls. Serve immediately or refrigerate.

Serves 6

Tapioca

When I was eleven years old or so, I got on a tapioca pudding kick when I went to visit my grandparents.

I made tapioca pudding for three years straight, at least seventy or eighty times. I used the quick-cooking Minute Tapioca that comes in the red box. It was a three-step process—cook in a saucepan, beat in the egg yolks, then fold in the whipped whites. I learned it. I got better with it. I started experimenting. I didn't know the chemistry behind it but I was good with flavor and texture. Eventually, I came up with an improved tapioca.

My grandfather would come home and see me and say, "Danny's here. I guess we're going to have tapioca pudding tonight." It was a foregone conclusion. The recipe made six servings. My grandmother would eat one; my grandfather would eat one; I'd eat four. That's just the way it worked out.

Many years later, the hotel threw a party to celebrate the tenth anniversary of the Boston Wine Festival, an annual series of food and wine dinners I started back in 1988. All my family—including my grandparents—were there, as well as local culinary luminaries like Julia Child. Dessert was tapioca pudding.

Vanilla-Poached Pears

One of the simpler desserts I make, these poached pears certainly don't lack for flavor, and the shape of the pear alone makes it beautiful to look at. Be careful not to buy overripe fruits—these are harder to poach. Mix any leftover poaching liquid with sparkling water for a delicious pick-me-up.

4 cups water

2 cups sugar

2 lemons, cut in half

1 tablespoon vanilla extract

6 cloves

1 cinnamon stick

6 pears (Bosc or Bartlett),
   peeled and cored

1. In a large saucepan over medium-high heat, bring the water, sugar, lemon halves, vanilla, cloves, and cinnamon stick to a boil. Reduce the heat to simmer and add the pears.

2. Cover the surface of the pan with a paper towel, lightly pressing the paper towel into the syrup. Simmer for 25 minutes or until the pears are easily pierced with a toothpick.

3. Serve warm with the poaching liquid or a scoop of vanilla ice cream.

Serves 6

DANIEL'S TIP:
You use a paper towel in this recipe so that the pears poach—not steam—and to prevent the fruit from turning color. Make sure the paper towel is moistened by the syrup.

Apple and Cranberry Brown Betty

This dish has been made in many variations since the colonial times. Reportedly it was President Ronald Reagan's favorite dessert—for good reason.

1. Preheat the oven to 375°F.

2. Using 1 teaspoon of the butter, grease an 8 x12-inch ovenproof casserole dish.

3. In a large sauté pan over medium-high heat, melt the remaining butter. When the butter starts to bubble, add the diced bread. Cook for 3½ minutes, tossing regularly to evenly toast the bread. Stir in the nutmeg and cinnamon. Continue toasting the bread for another 3–4 minutes, until it's crisp and golden. Set aside.

4. Meanwhile, in a bowl, toss together the apples, cranberries, brown sugar, and vanilla extract.

5. Place half the bread on the bottom of the buttered casserole dish. Evenly layer the apple mixture over the bread. Top with the remaining bread.

6. Cover with aluminum foil and bake for 45 minutes. Remove the foil and continue baking for an additional 20 minutes. Serve.

Serves 8

6 tablespoons (¾ stick) butter, melted, divided
12 slices white bread, diced (approximately 5 cups)
1 teaspoon nutmeg
1 teaspoon cinnamon
6 Granny Smith apples, peeled, cored, and thinly sliced
2 cups cranberries
1½ cups dark brown sugar
1 teaspoon vanilla extract

Deep-Dish Apple Pandowdy

This is really an upside-down apple pie. Some people like to push the pastry crust down once it comes out of the oven to soak up the apple juices. Try it with your favorite local baking apple.

Filling

2 teaspoons cornstarch

4 teaspoons water

⅓ cup maple syrup

¼ cup dark brown sugar

⅓ cup apple juice

½ teaspoon nutmeg

½ teaspoon cinnamon

¼ teaspoon salt

7 Gala apples, peeled, cored, and sliced

2 tablespoons butter, softened

1. Preheat the oven to 375°F.

2. In a small bowl, combine the cornstarch and water. Set aside.

3. In a saucepan over medium heat, bring the maple syrup, brown sugar, apple juice, nutmeg, cinnamon, and salt to a boil. Lower the heat to a simmer and whisk in the cornstarch mixture.

4. In a bowl, combine the apples and sauce.

5. Grease a 9 x 9-inch rectangular baking dish with the softened butter. Fill the dish with the apple mixture.

Pastry

2 cups all-purpose flour

¼ teaspoon salt

1 teaspoon baking powder

3 tablespoons sugar, divided

8 tablespoons (1 stick) cold butter, cut into thin slices

6 tablespoons cold milk

¾ teaspoon vanilla extract

1. Sift the flour, salt, baking powder, and 2 tablespoons of the sugar into a large bowl.

2. Add the butter and, using your fingers, work the butter into the flour until it forms almond-shaped slivers. Gently stir in the milk and vanilla to form a dough. Refrigerate the dough for 15 minutes.

3. On a floured work surface, roll out the dough to the same shape as the baking dish. Lay the dough on top of the apples; prick the entire surface with the tines of a fork, then sprinkle with the remaining tablespoon of sugar.

4. Bake for 50–55 minutes or until the pastry is golden brown. Cut into squares with a sharp knife and serve.

Serves 8

Peach Cobbler

Cobblers are baked, deep-dish fruit desserts with a dropped biscuit or crumb topping. Peaches or apricots are my favorite fruits for cobbler.

Fruit

5 fresh peaches
¾ cup sugar
Juice of 1 lemon
⅓ cup water, divided
2 tablespoons cornstarch

1. Preheat the oven to 375°F. Lightly butter an 8 x 10-inch ovenproof casserole.

2. Peel the peaches, cut them in half, remove the pits, and cut each of the halves into four wedges.

3. In a large saucepan over medium-high heat, bring the sliced peaches, sugar, lemon juice, and 2 tablespoons of the water to a gentle boil. Simmer for 2 minutes.

4. Dissolve the cornstarch in the remaining water and stir into the peaches. Simmer for 1 minute, then pour the mixture into the prepared casserole dish.

Batter

1 cup flour
1 teaspoon baking powder
¼ teaspoon salt
¾ teaspoon nutmeg
4 tablespoons (½ stick) soft butter
2 tablespoons sugar
1 egg
⅔ cup half-and-half

1. In a bowl, sift together the flour, baking powder, salt, and nutmeg.

2. In a second bowl, beat together the butter and sugar. Beat in the egg, followed by the sifted flour mixture and the half-and-half. Beat together until smooth, approximately 30 seconds.

3. Drop tablespoons of the batter over the peaches until the surface of the casserole is mostly covered. Bake for 35 minutes or until the top is golden brown.

4. Serve immediately with a dollop of whipped cream or vanilla ice cream.

Serves 8

Strawberry Shortcake with Cinnamon Whipped Cream

I've been perfecting this recipe ever since I was a kid and used to forage for the wild strawberries that grew near our house in Maine. If you can, serve the biscuits right out of the oven.

Biscuits

2 cups all-purpose flour

1 tablespoon baking powder

1 tablespoon sugar

4 tablespoons (½ stick) cold butter

¾ cup buttermilk

½ teaspoon vanilla extract

1. Preheat the oven to 375°F.

2. Sift the flour, baking powder, and sugar into a large bowl.

3. Cut the butter into paper-thin slices and gently stir into the flour mixture to preserve little bits of butter throughout the flour.

4. Make a well in the center of the flour and pour in the buttermilk and vanilla. Stir until the mixture forms a dough—and no longer.

5. On a well-floured work surface, roll the dough out ½ inch thick. Using a 2½-inch round biscuit or cookie cutter, cut the dough into eight circles. Carefully place the biscuits on a nonstick cookie sheet.

6. Bake for approximately 10 minutes or until the biscuits are a light brown.

1. Cut the berries into quarters and place them in a large bowl with the sugar and vanilla.

2. Toss the berries with the sugar and vanilla. Let sit at room temperature for at least 1 hour and up to 3 hours.

Place the cream, sugar, vanilla, and cinnamon into a chilled bowl and whip until the cream forms soft peaks.

1. Cut the biscuits in half. Arrange the biscuit bottoms in eight shallow bowls.

2. Divide the strawberries on top of the biscuit bottoms. Cover the berries with a biscuit top. Garnish with a dollop of whipped cream and optional confectioners' sugar and mint sprig.

Serves 8

Strawberries
1 quart fresh strawberries, washed and hulled
½ cup sugar
1 teaspoon vanilla extract

Whipped Cream
1 cup heavy cream
2 tablespoons sugar
½ teaspoon vanilla extract
¼ teaspoon cinnamon

Assembly
Confectioners' sugar (optional)
8 mint sprigs (optional)

DANIEL'S TIP:
When you're making whipped cream, if you use a chilled bowl and chilled beaters, the cream will whip more quickly. Even a few minutes in the freezer beforehand will speed along the process.

Raspberry Walnut Buckle

This is another one of those centuries-old desserts that are very popular in New England. I substitute walnuts and confectioners' sugar for the more traditional streusel topping—but the lemon is what really makes it pop.

8 tablespoons (1 stick) unsalted butter, softened
¾ cup sugar
1 teaspoon vanilla extract
Zest of 1 lemon
2 large eggs
½ cup sour cream
1½ cups all-purpose flour
1 teaspoon baking powder
½ teaspoon baking soda
¼ teaspoon salt
2 cups raspberries (about 2 half-pints)
1 cup walnut halves
1½ tablespoons confectioners' sugar

1. Preheat the oven to 350°F. Lightly butter an 8 x 8-inch ovenproof casserole dish.

2. In the bowl of an electric mixer with a paddle attachment or by hand using a spatula, beat together the butter and sugar until creamed. Add the vanilla, lemon zest, eggs, and sour cream.

3. Sift together the flour, baking powder, baking soda, and salt. Stir into the butter-and-sugar mixture. Mix until the batter is smooth, approximately 30 seconds.

4. Pour half of the raspberries evenly over the bottom of the casserole dish. Pour the batter evenly over the raspberries. Sprinkle with the walnuts and the remaining raspberries.

5. Bake for 35 minutes or until light brown and a toothpick inserted in the center comes out clean.

6. Remove from the oven, dust with confectioners' sugar, and serve.

Serves 6

No-Bake Blueberry Pie

Florence Blaisdell-Sterns used to make a version of this when I worked at her Candlelight restaurant in Skowhegan. She used to change out the berries, depending on the season.

Pastry

2 cups pastry flour
½ teaspoon salt
1 tablespoon sugar
8 tablespoons (1 stick) cold butter, cut into thin slices
3 tablespoons cold water
1 teaspoon white vinegar

1. Preheat the oven to 375°F.

2. Sift the flour, salt, and sugar into a large bowl.

3. Add the butter and, using your fingers, work the butter into the flour until it forms almond-shaped slivers. Gently stir in the water and vinegar to form a dough. Refrigerate the dough for 15 minutes.

4. On a floured work surface, roll out the dough into a 13-inch circle. Place the dough in a 10-inch pie plate, folding the edges over to cover the lip of the plate. Puncture the bottom and sides of the crust with the tines of a fork.

5. Place a second 10-inch pie plate over the dough. Bake for 40 minutes or until the crust is golden brown. Remove from the oven and carefully lift off the second pie plate.

Filling

4 cups (2 pints) fresh blueberries, washed and drained, divided
¾ cup water, divided
½ cup sugar
1 tablespoon fresh ginger juice (see Daniel's Tip)
Juice of 1 lemon
3 tablespoons cornstarch

1. Place 2½ cups of blueberries into a prebaked, 10-inch pie shell.

2. In small pan over medium-high heat, bring the remaining 1½ cups blueberries, ½ cup of the water, the sugar, ginger juice, and lemon juice to a boil. Lower the heat to a simmer.

3. In a small bowl, stir together the cornstarch and the remaining ¼ cup of water. Whisk this mixture into the simmering blueberries. Cook for an additional 1 minute then remove from the heat and strain through a strainer, pushing against the solids with the back of a spoon.

4. Immediately pour the strained liquid evenly over the blueberries in pie shell. Let set for 1 hour and serve.

Serves 8

DANIEL'S TIP:

Fresh ginger juice is a great addition to marinades and sauces. For 1 tablespoon ginger juice, place 3 tablespoons peeled, chopped ginger in a small saucepan with 1 tablespoon water. Bring to a boil, remove from the heat, and pour through a strainer, pressing against the solids with the back of a spoon.

Rhubarb and Oatmeal Crisp

Springtime in New England means rhubarb. While rhubarb is technically a vegetable, in 1947 a New York court declared it a fruit.

Rhubarb

1 cup sugar

5 cups washed and chopped rhubarb stalks

½ cup water, divided

3 tablespoons cornstarch

1. Preheat the oven to 350°F.

2. In a covered saucepan over medium-low heat, slowly cook the sugar, rhubarb, and half (¼ cup) of the water.

3. In a small bowl, dissolve the cornstarch in the remaining water. When the rhubarb starts to soften, stir in the cornstarch water. Simmer for 2 minutes then pour into an 8 x 8-inch ovenproof casserole dish.

Topping

1 cup rolled oats

½ cup brown sugar

8 tablespoons (1 stick) cold butter, cut into pieces

⅓ cup sifted flour

1 teaspoon cinnamon

½ teaspoon nutmeg

1 teaspoon vanilla extract

1. In a large bowl, mix together the oats, brown sugar, and butter until crumbly. Add the sifted flour, cinnamon, nutmeg, and vanilla; stir until just incorporated.

2. Sprinkle the topping evenly over the rhubarb. Bake for 35 minutes or until golden brown. Serve immediately.

Serves 8

Cherry and Plum Slump

Slump refers to the steamed dumplings that cover this classic dessert. When you remove the cover from the dish, the biscuits slightly collapse or "slump." Be sure to use a wide pan, large enough to hold the six dumplings.

Biscuits

1 cup all-purpose flour

1 teaspoon baking powder

3 tablespoons sugar

½ teaspoon nutmeg

½ teaspoon ground fennel

Pinch of salt

3 tablespoons cold butter, cut into small pieces

⅓ cup milk

1. Sift the flour, baking powder, sugar, nutmeg, ground fennel, and salt into a medium-sized bowl.

2. Add the butter and mix with your hands only until the butter crumbles to the size of peas.

3. Stir in the milk and mix until a batter begins to form. Don't overmix.

Fruit

4 plums, pitted and cut into quarters

1 cup cherries, pitted

½ cup sugar

1 teaspoon vanilla extract

¼ cup water

2 tablespoons chopped fresh mint

1. In a medium-sized saucepan, over medium-high heat, bring the plums, cherries, sugar, vanilla extract, and water to a boil. Lower the heat to a simmer, and simmer for 4 minutes. Stir in the mint.

2. Drop 6 tablespoons of the biscuit dough over the simmering fruit, allowing a small space between each spoonful of dough.

3. Cover and slowly simmer for 10 minutes. Serve immediately.

Serves 6

Pumpkin Indian Pudding

Is there any more quintessentially New England dessert than Indian pudding? Personally, I like it straight from the oven, in a bowl with a scoop of vanilla ice cream. I added the pumpkin because it contributes both moistness and flavor and deepens the already appetizingly orangey color of the dish.

1. Preheat the oven to 350°F.

2. In a large saucepan, bring the milk and butter to a gentle boil. Slowly whisk in the cornmeal. Simmer for 1 minute. Remove from the heat. Let cool for 15 minutes.

3. In a large bowl, combine the pumpkin puree, eggs, sugar, molasses, cinnamon, nutmeg, and salt. Pour in the cornmeal mixture and mix until smooth.

4. Pour the pudding into a buttered 9 x 9-inch baking dish. Place the dish into a larger roasting pan. Place the pan into oven. Pour in boiling water so that the water comes a quarter of the way up the sides of the dish.

5. Bake for 60 minutes. Remove from the oven and serve immediately with vanilla ice cream.

Serves 8

4 cups whole milk
¼ cup (½ stick) butter
½ cup cornmeal, white or yellow
1 cup pumpkin puree (canned is fine)
4 eggs
¼ cup sugar
¾ cup dark molasses
1 teaspoon cinnamon
1 teaspoon nutmeg
¼ teaspoon salt

Baked Hazelnut and Ginger Cake

This is a very moist cake that still holds up well several days after baking. It has a distinct but gentle ginger flavor.

⅔ cup peeled and finely chopped fresh ginger

⅔ cup vegetable oil

⅔ cup sugar

⅔ cup molasses

½ teaspoon salt

1¾ cups sifted all-purpose flour

1 teaspoon baking soda

1 teaspoon cinnamon

¼ teaspoon ground cloves

½ teaspoon black pepper

2 eggs

¾ cup chopped hazelnuts (or walnuts)

1. Preheat the oven to 325°F.

2. Place the ginger, oil, sugar, molasses, and salt in the bowl of a food processor. Pulse until fully incorporated.

3. Place the ginger mixture into a bowl. Add the flour, baking soda, cinnamon, cloves, and black pepper. Beat for 1 minute.

4. Beat in the eggs, then fold in the hazelnuts. Pour the batter into a lightly greased 10 x 10-inch ovenproof baking dish, individual ramekins, or mini fluted cake pans.

5. Bake for 35 minutes (a few minutes less for individual pans) or until a toothpick inserted into the center comes out clean. Let rest for 5 minutes before serving. Garnish with whipped cream.

Serves 4

Cocoa Bread Pudding

Everyone loves bread pudding. I don't think there is a better way to use stale bread. Don't limit yourself to white bread—any bread will do.

1. Preheat the oven to 350°F.

2. Lightly butter a 3-quart or 9 x 9-inch ovenproof casserole dish with the tablespoon of butter. Spread the bread cubes evenly over the bottom of the dish.

3. In a bowl, beat together the eggs, sugar, and cocoa powder until smooth. Stir in the milk, cream, and vanilla. Pour the mixture over the cubed bread. Lightly push down the bread so that all of it is covered by liquid.

4. Place the casserole in a roasting pan and into the oven. Fill the pan with water a quarter of the way up the sides of the casserole.

5. Bake the pudding for 45 minutes or until it's springy to the touch.

6. Meanwhile, melt the bittersweet chocolate in the top of a double boiler over simmering water.

7. Drizzle the melted chocolate over the bread pudding, cut into squares, and immediately serve.

Serves 6

1 tablespoon butter
2 cups cubed stale white bread
5 eggs
½ cup sugar
⅓ cup cocoa powder
2½ cups milk
½ cup heavy cream
½ teaspoon vanilla extract
¼ cup bittersweet chocolate

Chocolate Flourless Cake with Sour Cream and Berries

The spiced fruit adds another dimension to this wonderful dessert.

⅓ cup bittersweet chocolate
8 tablespoons (1 stick)
   butter
¾ cup sugar, divided
3 eggs, separated
⅔ cup cocoa powder,
   divided
½ cup sour cream
½ teaspoon allspice
1 tablespoon honey
1 cup assorted fresh berries
   (raspberries, blueberries,
   strawberries, or a
   combination)

1. Preheat the oven to 350°F.

2. Lightly grease a 10-inch cake pan with cooking spray.

3. In the top of a double boiler over simmering water, melt the chocolate and the butter, stirring often until smooth.

4. Remove from the heat, then beat in ½ cup of the sugar, the egg yolks, and ½ cup of the cocoa powder.

5. In a separate bowl, whisk the egg whites. When the whites get frothy, slowly add the remaining sugar and continue whisking until the egg whites form soft peaks. Fold the whites into the batter with a spatula.

6. Pour the batter evenly into the prepared cake pan and bake for 25 minutes or until a toothpick inserted in the center comes out clean.

7. Let the cake cool for 5 minutes. Carefully unmold onto waxed paper, then gently flip it onto a serving dish with the crust side up.

8. In a small bowl, mix together the sour cream, allspice, honey, and berries.

9. Lightly dust the cake with the remaining cocoa powder and serve with the sour cream and berries.

Serves 4

Boston Cream Pie

Contrary to what you may think, this is actually a cake, not a pie. Created in Boston almost 150 years ago, this dish is also the official dessert of the state of Massachusetts.

Cake

2 eggs, separated
1½ cups sugar, divided
2¼ cups cake flour
1 tablespoon baking
   powder
1 teaspoon salt
⅓ cup canola oil
1 cup milk
1 teaspoon vanilla extract

1. Preheat the oven to 350°F. Grease and lightly flour a 9-inch cake pan.

2. In a medium-sized bowl, beat the egg whites with an electric mixer Gradually add ½ cup of the sugar, until stiff peaks form.

3. In a second, larger bowl, sift together the remaining cup of sugar, the cake flour, baking powder, and salt. Add the oil, milk, egg yolks, and vanilla. Beat for 1 minute at medium speed.

4. Scrape down the sides of the bowl with a spatula. Gently fold in the egg whites.

5. Pour the mixture into the prepared cake pan. Bake for about 35–40 minutes or until a toothpick inserted into the center comes out clean.

6. Cool the cake for 10 minutes, then carefully remove it from the pan by inverting the cake onto a cake rack or waxed paper.

7. When it's thoroughly cool, cut the cake into two equally thick disks. Line the cake pan with plastic wrap and return the lower disk to the pan. Set the top disk aside.

Cream Filling

1⅓ cups milk, divided
⅓ cup sugar
1 egg, beaten
¼ cup cornstarch
1 tablespoon butter
1 teaspoon vanilla extract

1. In a saucepan over medium heat, heat 1 cup of the milk and the sugar until the milk comes to a simmer.

2. In a bowl, mix together the remaining ⅓ cup milk, the egg, and the cornstarch. Stirring vigorously, slowly pour the hot milk into the cornstarch mixture. When the milk is thoroughly combined, pour the mixture back into the pot and return to the heat, stirring constantly until the mixture thickens and boils.

3. Cook and stir for 1 more minute, then remove from the heat. Stir in the butter and vanilla.

4. Let the filling cool for 10 minutes. Then pour the mixture evenly over the cake disk in the pan. Top with the second cake disk. Gently press down, cover, and refrigerate for at least 2 hours and as long as 24 hours.

Assembly

⅓ cup semisweet chocolate
2 tablespoons butter
1 teaspoon vanilla extract
1 tablespoon heavy cream

1. In a double boiler over low heat, melt the chocolate and butter, stirring constantly.

2. Remove from the heat and stir in the vanilla and heavy cream until smooth.

3. Carefully remove the cake from the pan. Place the cake on a cake stand or decorative plate. Pour the melted chocolate over the top center of the cake and serve.

Serves 8

DANIEL'S TIP:
If you're feeling fancy, you can melt a quarter cup of white chocolate in the top of a double boiler and drizzle it over the top of the frosted cake in four concentric circles. Lightly pull a small knife in eight "spokes" from the center of the cake to the edge to form the decorative pattern.

ACKNOWLEDGMENTS

A book is not written in a vacuum. There have been supporters and advisors all along the way, who deserve my thanks and acknowledgement.

Thank you to my legion of recipe testers for giving me such terrific feedback and insight. Bob Butera, Marilyn Sifford, Barbara Ferriter and Ned Whitmore, Ken Butera and Carol Wasylyshyn, Rena Coen, Liz and Sean Greenhalgh, and France Posener each tried a few recipes and supplied useful feedback. Mimi and Reuben Kantor, Carol and Howie Rubin, Maria Maffei, and Eugene Ferriter tested several with valuable results. Rachel and Stephen Kent, Glenn Selmi, Amy and John Pironti, marvelous cooks all, kept coming back for more. Megan Mear, the first to begin testing, is in a league of her own. She is always there for my

family and me. Jody and Erik Saarma were dedicated to the caus
detailed feedback and questions. Teryn and Karl Weintz, cha
of testing, took it on like a challenge and returned photos and
commentary on more than a third of the recipes in this bool
you to all; I hope you enjoyed the tasty rewards. I so appreciate you
invaluable help.

I have been gratified for over twenty-five years to work as the executive chef of the Boston Harbor Hotel. It is always new and rewarding.
My staff's dedication and pride in their work inspire me every day. Pyramid Advisors has given me facilities, freedom, and support to create
and grow in my field, as well as produce this book.

Mat Schaffer and I have been friends for more than twenty years.
We figured this out together. Our friendship enabled us to create a pro-
ductive working relationship that produced this book.

Our agent Jennifer Griffin of the Miller Bowers Griffin Agency
believed in this project from the beginning. Jim Grace of the Arts &
Business Council of Greater Boston generously offered us his legal
expertise and advice. Thank you both.

Ron Manville and I have worked together and talked about this
book for years. Thanks to his stunning images, we finally did it!

I'd like to thank Mary Norris, our editor, who has made this process
so easy and pleasant. She is has been there every step of the way to guide
and instruct us. She has made this first effort a pleasure.

My wonderful children, Charlotte and Elliot, have grown up eating
many of these dishes. Sharing meals with my children and my wife has
been at the core of our close family life.

METRIC CONVERSION TABLES

Metric–U.S. Approximate Equivalents

Liquid Ingredients

METRIC	U.S. MEASURES	METRIC	U.S. MEASURES
1.23 ML	¼ TSP.	29.57 ML	2 TBSP.
2.36 ML	½ TSP.	44.36 ML	3 TBSP.
3.70 ML	¾ TSP.	59.15 ML	¼ CUP
4.93 ML	1 TSP.	118.30 ML	½ CUP
6.16 ML	1¼ TSP.	236.59 ML	1 CUP
7.39 ML	1½ TSP.	473.18 ML	2 CUPS OR 1 PT.
8.63 ML	1¾ TSP.	709.77 ML	3 CUPS
9.86 ML	2 TSP.	946.36 ML	4 CUPS OR 1 QT.
14.79 ML	1 TBSP.	3.79 L	4 QTS. OR 1 GAL.

Dry Ingredients

METRIC	U.S. MEASURES	METRIC		U.S. MEASURES
2 (1.8) G	¹⁄₁₆ OZ.	80 G		2⅘ OZ.
3½ (3.5) G	⅛ OZ.	85 (84.9) G		3 OZ.
7 (7.1) G	¼ OZ.	100 G		3½ OZ.
15 (14.2) G	½ OZ.	115 (113.2) G		4 OZ.
21 (21.3) G	¾ OZ.	125 G		4½ OZ.
25 G	⅞ OZ.	150 G		5¼ OZ.
30 (28.3) G	1 OZ.	250 G		8⅞ OZ.
50 G	1¾ OZ.	454 G	1 LB.	16 OZ.
60 (56.6) G	2 OZ.	500 G	1 LIVRE	17⅗ OZ.

INDEX

ABOUT THE AUTHORS

Daniel Bruce is executive chef at the Boston Harbor Hotel, where he founded the annual Boston Wine Festival (www.bostonwinefestival. net) and oversees all dining operations, including Meritage restaurant (www.meritagetherestaurant.com) and the Rowes Wharf Sea Grille. Daniel is also culinary consultant for Pyramid Hotel Group and has founded and overseen Wine Festivals in New Orleans, Berkeley, and Washington, DC. Annually, more than six hundred thousand people dine in these venues, with over three hundred thousand at the Boston Harbor Hotel alone.

Daniel has been profiled in the *New York Times, New York Post, Boston Globe, Boston Herald, Wall Street Journal, Newsday, Chicago Sun-Times, Providence Journal, USA Today, Bon Appétit, Boston* magazine, *BusinessWeek, Cuisiner, Fitness, Food Arts, Food Illustrated, Food & Wine, Good Housekeeping, Gourmet, Health, Home & Garden, New England Travel Guide, Quarterly Review of Wines, Sante, Travel + Leisure, Wine & Food Companion,* and *Wine Spectator.* He has cooked on the *Today* show, *Regis & Kelly,* the *Tom Snyder Show, Simply Ming,* and virtually every television station in New England. International television includes segments for the BBC as well as Italian and Irish television.

In 2012 the *Boston Globe* described Daniel as "maybe the best chef in town." He has been recognized twice as one of the Best Hotel Chefs in America by the James Beard Foundation; has been awarded the title of Vice Conseiller Culinaire, Bailliage de Boston by La Chaine des Rotisseurs; is an honorary member of Chevaliers du Tastevin; and has received an honorary doctorate degree from his alma mater, J&W University. In 2013 he was honored as "Chef of the Year" by the Massachusetts Restaurant Association. He grew up in New England and lives with his family in Boston, Massachusetts.

Mat Schaffer is the former restaurant critic and food editor of the *Boston Herald* and the former restaurant critic for *Boston* magazine. He has written for *Food & Wine, Simply Seafood, Food Illustrated, Wine Spectator, Cigar Aficionado, Metropolitan Home, Boston Common,* and *Where* magazines and online at epicurious.com. He lives in Boston, Massachusetts. matschafferconsulting.com